Rehabilitation and deviance

Philip Bean

*Department of
Applied Social Science
University of Nottingham*

Routledge & Kegan Paul
London and Boston

First published in 1976
by Routledge & Kegan Paul Ltd
Broadway House, 68-74 Carter Lane,
London EC4V 5EL and
9 Park Street,
Boston, Mass. 02108, USA
Set in IBM Press Roman by
Pentagon Print
and printed in Great Britain by
Redwood Burn Ltd
Trowbridge & Esher

ISBN 0 7100 8270 3 (c)
     0 7100 8271 1 (p)

CONTENTS

To Amy, Nita and Trevor

Preface and acknowledgments

It is not very fashionable for sociologists nowadays to be involved in social engineering; a more lofty detachment seems to be preferred. Yet in a curious way that same lofty detachment is a hallmark of other groups who are not always given the warmest of welcomes in sociological circles and who, like many sociologists, are not really detached at all. Detachment is all very well, but Howard Becker's pertinent question forces us to reappraise our position from time to time. Becker wanted to know 'whose side are we on?' and the answer is I suppose likely to change at frequent intervals. In this book, I have unashamedly adopted a social engineering approach and, as will be clear from the following pages, I am not always on the side of the rehabilitationists. My position is this, that rehabilitation as it is practised in the modern penal system is not what it seems to be, and on closer examination is often incompatible with current penal aims. I can only offer tentative suggestions as to where we go from there, and hopefully others will pick up the argument and bring the debate into the open. For too long the arguments about the penal system have been assessed on the basis of labels; supporters of rehabilitation have regarded with intense suspicion anyone who opposed it, whilst opponents have regarded the other side with equal doubts. Labels seem to me to be a poor way of arriving at rational decisions.

Throughout this venture Professor David Marsh provided encouragement, assistance and inspiration, as did those who kindly read the drafts. I want to record sincere thanks to two highly perceptive sociologists, Meryl Horrocks and Alan Aldridge at the University of Nottingham who read and commented on the drafts; to Herschel Prins at the School of

Social Work, University of Leicester, who carefully read the drafts and who made more valuable criticisms than I dare remember. Also, I want to give special thanks to the series editor, Professor Vic George, University of Kent, who made another set of valuable and important comments. Valerie, my wife, has had all the arguments presented on countless occasions and has fortunately remained sceptical throughout. Christine Woolley and Joanna Fisher typed the drafts in a speedy and efficient manner, and to those mentioned above and to countless others, I would like to express my special gratitude.

The author and publisher would like to thank the following for permission to reproduce copyright material: HMSO for Tables 3.1 and 3.2 from 'Preliminary Report on the Probationary Research Project 1966'; Basic Books Inc. for the extract from 'On Record: Files and Dossiers in American Life', edited by Stanton Wheeler © 1969 by Russell Sage Foundation, on pp.106-7; and the American Correctional Association for the extract from 'Manual of Correctional Standards', on pp.117-18.

Rehabilitation – AN OVERVIEW

This book is about the penal system as it exists in England and Wales in the 1970s. It is also about rehabilitation which, in the context of the modern penal system, means being sentenced to receive help. Sentences to receive help are now so much part of the judicial and penal process, that we now regard them as common practice. Occasionally judges and magistrates pass a sentence for different reasons — retributive or as a deterrent perhaps — but officials operating the penal processes invariably attempt to turn the sentence into a rehabilitative one. We think there is nothing strange about this apparent conflict. We also accept that a sentence to be helped can be passed on all types of offenders, in all age groups, and for almost all types of offences ranging from driving with no 'L' plates to homicide. And yet seventy-five years ago, the Gladstone Committee thought it no concern of the penal system to be involved in the rehabilitation of offenders.[1] How then has rehabilitation become so important, or to put the question another way, what is meant by rehabilitation, and how does it operate in the courts and in the penal system? The time now seems right to begin to ask these questions in a systematic way, for ideas about rehabilitation have wider implications than issues about the treatment of offenders.

Although the central concern in this book is rehabilitation as it affects the modern penal system, juvenile offenders have not been included. Juvenile justice is now changing rapidly. The recent Children and Young Persons Act 1969 contains many radical proposals, not all of which have been implemented, but if and when they are, there will be two separate systems of justice operating in the courts. There will be

1

one for adults which will place more emphasis on legal requirements and be primarily concerned with legal rights and duties. It will be operated by traditional groups such as police, magistrates, judges, etc. The other will be for juveniles which will emphasize the social background of the offenders and be operated primarily by social workers. Such a change requires, I think, a separate analysis.

By confining the analysis to adult offenders — which in this context means those aged 17 and over — other complications are conveniently avoided. Special legal and penal provisions existed for juveniles long before the 1969 Act was introduced. They separated juveniles from adult offenders and placed juveniles in a special legal category. The venue for the trial is different, and there is a legal age of criminal responsibility which was fixed at 7 years in 1908, is now 10, and the 1969 Act gives power to raise it to 14. If a juvenile commits an offence below the age of criminal responsibility there is a presumption that he cannot tell the difference between right and wrong.[2] Between the ages of 10 and 14 juveniles are in a twilight zone in which they are morally responsible not as a group but as individuals when they know their acts to be wrong.[3] They are presumed in this age group to be in 'doli incapax' — or ignorant of the wrongfulness of the act. The presumption is refutable, and in practice varies from court to court, some courts virtually ignoring it altogether — but its very existence presupposes that juveniles entering the penal system are qualitatively different from adults.

Similarly penal provisions for juveniles have always been more varied and elaborate. Some, such as borstals and detention centres, continue to take adult offenders up to the age of 21 but above that age courts had until recently only four major alternatives for sentencing: discharges, fines, probation and prison. The range for juveniles has always been wider and was justified on the grounds that penal resources ought to be directed at the young, particularly as the evidence suggested that adult offenders were almost always drawn from the ranks of the juvenile delinquents. Incidentally the position has changed in the last decade and fewer adult recidivists have been convicted by the juvenile courts.

I am not suggesting that juvenile justice should be different from adult justice, merely that it is now, and is likely to continue to be so in the future. Hopefully many of the points raised here will be applicable to any subsequent analysis of the juvenile courts, as the 1969 Act raises issues about rehabilitation in a particularly acute form. Juveniles more than any other age group are subject to the professional helpers, with all the attendant trappings of casework and psychotherapy.

Having cleared some of the ground as far as juveniles are concerned, further provisos need to be added. The aim is not to describe the penal system or even concentrate on the mechanics of it, but to analyse one particular approach, or ideology, which comes under the general heading of reform or rehabilitation. Following Francis Allen I shall call it the 'rehabilitative ideal'.[4] I shall be concerned with examining this ideal as a concept, and to show how, if at all, it has been successfully used to combat crime and recidivism. Inevitably this will involve discussing it in generalities, and no apology is made for that approach. It will also involve general questions about how and why rehabilitation is now regarded as a self evident good, and why there has been so little discussion about some of the underlying principles, or even its overall effects. Why, for example, does a challenge to the rehabilitative position often bring forth a whole series of pejorative labels such as 'reactionary', 'inhuman' and 'punitive'? I hope to show that these labels may well be misapplied and might even be more applicable to the labellers than the labelled.

It may still seem a little surprising that a critical examination of the rehabilitative ideal could be a suitable subject for a series on radical social policy. The stereotype of the radical in this particular field is as a supporter of rehabilitation. The recent spate of cases involving the abduction of babies illustrates this point. The 'radicals' argued for a more treatment orientated approach, whilst the 'reactionaries' wanted prison sentences. But in one sense it all depends what one means by 'radical'. Inkeri Anttila in a perceptive essay makes the point that those supporting the rehabilitative ideal may now find themselves less radical than they supposed.

> The *avant garde* position has become more complicated. Some of those who have previously considered themselves radical in their demands for a constantly more treatment orientated criminal policy have now noticed in the eyes of other radicals they are now perhaps almost conservative in that they defend the traditional thesis that criminals shall first of all have treatment.[5]

Although the term radical may mean as much as one wants it to mean, we can think of it as being used in arguments about change, and profound change at that. By this definition, a critique of rehabilitation becomes essentially radical, for rehabilitation has already achieved an entrenched and established position. Support can be found amongst more powerful sections of our society and amongst groups who would not usually find themselves in ideological harmony. In evidence submitted to the Royal Commission on the Penal System[6] various bodies openly supported the rehabilitative ideal. These, to name but a few, included the British Medical Association, the Fabian Society, the Institute of Psychiatry, the Society of Labour Lawyers and the National Association for Mental Health.[7] Numerous private individuals in their evidence also supported rehabilitation; these included magistrates, doctors and politicians.

The rehabilitative ideal is also supported by the mass media, the more fashionable 'quality' papers and most of the learned journals. Until recently almost all criminological texts had an implicit reformist approach, whilst some criminologists explicitly argued for more rehabilitation; they wanted more treatment facilities, more social workers and more psychiatrists to treat even more offenders. It is difficult to gauge the extent of their influence but they did have a ready access to the mass media, so their influence could have been considerable.

Within the penal system itself there is almost total agreement about the value of rehabilitation, although perhaps one should be wary of accepting some of these views at face value. The Prison Officers' Association has asked for more rehabilitation and wants to become more involved in the treatment of prisoners, so do the Governor grades within the prisons. The Probation and After-Care Service is an overt supporter of rehabilitation − in fact probation training consists of little else. The judiciary at all levels occasionally sentence along rehabilitative lines. Had juveniles been included in this essay the list could have been extended to cover Social Services Departments, the majority of juvenile court magistrates, and the police in their capacity as juvenile liaison officers. When Inkeri Anttila wrote of a 'breakthrough' for the reformist position, she was directing attention at the potential power and the actual influence of groups supporting reform. She was also right to draw attention to the extent and speed with which reform has gained ground in what she calls 'a thorough all pervading manner and in a remarkably short space of time considering the usual rate of change within a penal system'. In short, rehabilitation has been generally accepted as a legitimate way of dealing with adult offenders.

Having become accepted, even if not wholly practised, the effects of rehabilitation are far reaching. But before discussing the more pertinent issues, we need first to begin to clear some of the conceptual ground. The first problem is a definitional one, as the term 'rehabilitation' is now so widely used as to make almost all existing definitions either too wide or too narrow to be workable. The first point, then, is more of a warning than an explanation, and a warning against being misled by what Francis Allen calls 'the delusive simplicity and ambiguity of the notion of reform'.[8] In other words, it all sounds simple and appealing until one looks closely at the concepts. Furthermore, key words used in the definitions are often used interchangeably and rarely with precision; 'diagnosis', 'needs' and 'therapy' being the more obvious examples. A persistent source of confusion is the frequent failure to distinguish between 'treatment' and 'training' as well as between 'reform' and 'rehabilitation'. To clarify the last set of terms, the distinction made by Roger Hood is a useful one at this stage. He thinks 'training means a conscious effort to influence the attitudes of others, whilst "treatment" seems to imply a method of dealing with the problems of the individual offender'.[9] The first is related to *external* impositions or *external* control, the latter means the *internalization* of values probably acquired through contact with a significant other, e.g. a therapist. This seems a workable distinction, although it is the term 'treatment' that concerns us most. As far as 'rehabilitation' and 'reform' are concerned we shall use these interchangeably, although doubtless fine distinctions could be drawn.

Second, whilst acknowledging the warning of Francis Allen, we need a workable definition which can be related to current usage. The workable definition has been provided by Plato when he said 'The State should stand in *loco parentis*. Wickedness is a mental disease, disintegrating and ultimately fatal.'[10] The modern version is, however, more complex, as wickedness, or crime, for our purposes may often be seen as a mental disease but more likely as a form of maladjustment. The term maladjustment has its own special definitional problems.

However, two examples will hopefully illustrate how the term rehabilitation is currently used. Both quotes are taken from the Royal Commission on the penal system and both are from the evidence given by the Medical Officer at Feltham Borstal.

Although at the present state of our understanding and knowledge the mental attitudes and behaviour patterns of [criminals] are not the same as those of people who are mentally ill, yet it cannot be denied that their mental characteristics are abnormal, in fact diseased.

Once the disease model is accepted, diagnosis follows.

If crime is to be understood and recidivism prevented the first essential in the public's interest is that the mind of the individual be studied and its difference in function from the normal mind of the socially conforming should be understood.[11]

A magistrate, also giving evidence, invokes the maladjustment argument;

The underlying cause of the problem of delinquency is maladjustment . . . .[12]

There is no equivocation about the magistrate's position, although the quotes from the medical officer are for our purposes the more interesting. They are extraordinary in a number of respects. First they illustrate the point that terms are used to support the main argument which are wholly contentious yet are presented almost as value free concepts, apparently selected for their scientific precision. But what, for example, does the 'normal mind of the socially conforming' mean? Each word of that clause could lead to a separate discussion in itself. The statement by the magistrate poses the obvious question, maladjusted to what? Presumably to the socially conforming, and that is equally contentious. Furthermore, what is 'the underlying cause' supposed to mean? Notice also that the medical officer asks for more research to enable distinctions to be made between the criminal and non-criminal. Demands for this type of positivist research are a recurrent theme within the reformist position.

Plato, having invoked the disease concept, then logically moves to the next stage and asserts the need for treatment: 'No punishment inflicted by law is for the sake of harm but to make the sufferer better, or to make him less bad than he would have been without it.' The Fabian Society would agree, 'We are convinced of the sterility of the punitive-retributive attitude which still pervades in our courts.' The answer then is more rehabilitation; 'We should like to see not only a full-scale Family Service doing effective pre-delinquency, but also [penal institutions], turned into genuine treatment centres where residents would receive individual attention and where treatment would be flexible.'[13] The American Correctional Association shows how such a policy ought to operate. 'The modern philosophy of rehabilitation is put to practical application by the development of three related and continuous phases of the correctional process; probation, institutional training and treatment, and parole.'[14] In other words, rehabilitation should extend throughout the whole of the penal system, with the Fabian Society making it clear that courts should not adopt a punitive-retributive attitude under any circumstances. In Plato's words, they want the diseased to be made better.

These quotes also highlight a number of other features of the reformist position. Apart from the constant demands for more research, there is always the explicit use of medical terms such as diagnosis and treatment. There is also the inherent attack on any other ideology which is regarded as punitive. (The word 'punitive' has now acquired its own pejorative overtones and is used as an attacking label.) Finally, the problem of crime is said to be found within the psychology of the criminal. Plato did not say that *crime* was a disease but the *criminal* was diseased. The difference is crucial, for emphasis is then placed on the offender, with little questioning of the social system or of the experts who define that disease.

Crime as a social problem is seen by the reformist largely in psychological/psychiatric terms. This is no accident, although sociologists have been reformists, too. Whereas psychiatrists talk in terms of internal conflicts, etc., sociologists have stressed defective socialization, criminal role models and alternative opportunity structures. Their influence, however, has never been as widespread. There are numerous reasons for this, not the least being that sociology does not lend itself so easily to treatment plans. Although sociologists may have some part to play in the 'diagnosis', the psychiatric approach has all the built-in advantages when it comes to personal treatment.

Finally, before moving to the main thrust of the argument there are two other issues which need some consideration. They need consideration because the terminology used has the great disadvantage — or advantage — of glossing over certain contradictory positions.

The first is primarily philosophical and concerns the question of whether reform *accompanies* punishment or whether it *results* from punishment.[15] Detention in a psychiatric hospital may not of itself be an essential part of curing mental disorders, but it may provide a convenient opportunity for psychotherapy. In this instance reform accompanies punishment, as reform operates by exploiting the opportunities presented by compulsory detention. An offender required to report to a probation officer or a psychiatrist is in a similar position. He is attending under legal compulsion, and reform accompanies the compulsion. On the other hand, reformists are offering a theory of punishment if they say that a person has been reformed as a result of losing his liberty or having to attend the probation office. If loss of liberty is said to lead to reform it becomes a theory of punishment as it implies that loss of liberty has certain intrinsic moral qualities which have produced the change in behaviour.

Presumably most reformists accept that within the penal system there will be an element of compulsion and presumably reformists are not arguing that loss of liberty or other forms of compulsion lead to reform. They want, or expect, reform to accompany some form of punishment. In this sense probation is no less a punishment than prison, for both contain elements of compulsion and both could accompany reform. It is no less a punishment because an offender agrees to be placed on probation, particularly as the courts do not spell out the alternatives if he refuses. On this basis, when rehabilitation is discussed within the context of the penal system it is always discussed in relation to the way it accompanies punishment. The difference is crucial, for demands for more reform implicitly accept some elements of punishment. The American Correctional Association, as an ardent advocate of reform, walks round this dilemma, or at least tries not to notice it.

The position taken by proponents of the theory of rehabilitation may be summed up as follows: — They do not rule out the necessity of custodial segregation but consider custody a means to an end in the vast majority of cases, and an end in very few cases. They do not deny the desirability of achieving a deterrent effect if it can be done without impairing the effectiveness of rehabilitative programmes . . .[16]

In other words reform should accompany punishment and deterrence can be introduced occasionally if it is functionally part of a reformist programme.

The second confusion is less philosophical, more political. One of the main strands of the reformist position is that reform is claimed to be a humanitarian philosophy. The term is used here in the sense of 'humanizing' rather than as a systematic ideology, although often it is difficult to decide if humanitarian means nothing more than leniency and shorter sentences. However, the reformists have fostered the humanitarian argument as a buttress against other philosophies. Reformists point to the lack of concern for the offender's welfare under retributionist and utilitarian regimes and compare the considerable improvements in penal conditions since the reformist lobby began to exert an influence. Up to a point there is some force in this argument. Probation after all received some of its ideological thrust as a result of the appalling conditions within prisons. Punishments were often excessive, often barbaric and conditions in penal colonies were grossly inhuman. Retributionists have been overconcerned with deserts; and utilitarians themselves rarely questioned the treadmill or the silent system in prisons except to ask about their efficacy as deterrents. With the treadmill the debate was about the number of revolutions required each day; and with the silent system it was based on the need to provide time to brood and think, although as one wag remarked all could brood but regrettably not all could think. Nevertheless, the prisoners' welfare was secondary to other major aims.

The lack of direct concern for the offender is of course built in to the theoretical models of these philosophies. This means that by default they have handed the humanitarian argument to the reformists. Recently there has been some attempt to regain the initiative when those advocating deterrence or retribution claim to represent the interests of the victim, although this does not appear to have been a particularly successful form of attack. This is not to deny some merit in the argument, for the reformist position *does* ignore the victim and concern for the offender's welfare has not produced a similar concern for the victim. We then have the extraordinary position of supporters of reform claiming to represent one set of humanitarian interests with opponents claiming to represent another. Both claim to be humanitarian.

To link the growth of humanitarianism with the influence of the rehabilitative ideal is misleading in another more fundamental sense, for it assumes that they moved in a direct relationship with each other.

This is not to say that reform has not had some influence, although it is inconceivable that to modern society with its abhorrence of physical pain the punishments of the eighteenth century would still be permitted, and only in penal institutions at that. More likely there was a trend away from inhuman conditions and the reformist position arose at the same time as this general trend. Furthermore, another misleading approach is to present the rehabilitative ideal as part of an evolutionary process, with its attendant implications of progress. The American Correctional Association exemplifies this point. Earlier sections of this report trace the history of punishment and note the inhumanity of nineteenth century penal policy. Suddenly inhumanity vanishes but exactly at the point where the reformists enter the picture. Although the report does not actually say the reformists were solely responsible for the change the implication is there, and the presentation of this type of historical cataloguing feeds the implication. It also suggests that an even higher point in the evolutionary process will be reached when all penal institutions become committed to reform.

There are two serious flaws here. The first is that humanitarian considerations are linked with the reformist process although they are analytically separate. An example will help clarify the point. Prisoners have recently been granted periods of free association at certain selected periods when they can talk, play table tennis, etc. But free association of itself is not a reformist measure *unless* it is expected to lead to changes in attitude about crime or it is part of a wider rehabilitative programme. We cannot, as Richard Cloward points out, claim that humanistic exercises are automatically reformative.[17] Invariably, no such programme exists but the assumption is made that free association somehow automatically leads to reform. This assumption lacks empirical foundations as free association is nothing more than a way of alleviating boredom in prisons — a very good idea but hardly re-formative in this context.

The second flaw is more serious. It has become so easy to equate humanitarian consideration with rehabilitation that we forget that they may often conflict; that they rarely do is because of the safeguards provided by a strong component of retributive justice in our penal system. The problem is simply this. If the offence is to be ignored, perhaps because of the difficulties in determining blameworthiness or desert, the sentence is then based on the 'needs' of the offender. Needs obviously differ and so conceivably a murderer and a parking offender could both serve prison sentences for their offence, both having a need for imprisonment but the murderer having fewer needs is let out earlier. It is equally conceivable that the murderer could be placed on pro-bation, and the parking offender sent to prison. Reformists usually object to this type of argument on the grounds that anyone committing murder is likely to have more 'needs' anyway. This is a circular argument for 'needs' are then determined by the offence and the offence defines the 'needs'. Futhermore, we are back to a form of retributive justice in any case as the murderer's needs are based on the offence and he will be expected to stay in prison longer because his needs, defined by the offence, are greater.

Professor Flew does not think that anyone could complain that for Plato the thesis that all crime is an expression of psychological disease constitutes what he calls a 'Mollycoddlers Charter'.[18] Neither does Professor Glueck who is an ardent advocate of reform. Under a reformist regime,

> an offender will not know in advance of his crime just how long he will have to be under correctional control and subject to therapeutic intervention; and in fact certain offenders may have to remain under control for a longer term than if the sentence had been legislatively fixed or narrowly restricted in advance.[19]

George Jackson's case illustrates the point. In 1960 Jackson, at the age of 18, was convicted of second degree robbery for driving a get-away car while a friend robbed a petrol station of seventy dollars. Under the Californian State Law, which claims to have the most advanced reformists penal code, Jackson and his accomplice were sentenced to a period of between one year and life imprisonment. After serving the first year the parole board determines when the prisoner should be released on parole. Under that system, parole is granted when the board thinks a prisoner has been sufficiently reformed to be let out. Jackson's accomplice was released in 1963, Jackson remained until 1970 and subsequently died in prison.[20] He claimed his political beliefs prevented him from being granted parole — he was a black revolutionary — and as long as he expounded those beliefs he was not considered reformed. The only sure chance for Jackson was, as he claimed, to reduce his individuality and appear to be like everyone else for to be different is seen as synonymous to having 'needs' and 'problems'. Jackson refused to compromise.

Reformists, who shift attention to the offender rather than consider the crime must, if they are to accept the logic of their position, withdraw all retributive limitation. The length of time to be spent in institutions becomes dependent on a board comprised of experts who claim to know when reform has been achieved. Whether this is humanitarian is something else again although it seems that humanitarianism means something more than inflicting pain — it means something to do with Justice and other non-psychological terms. In Selznick's phrase, justice must serve the proper ends of man. In George Jackson's case justice did not mean spending ten years in prison waiting to be pronounced reformed by a body of experts. This point will be examined in detail later; at this stage we can note that decisions about the nature of reform are another part of the deceptive simplicity of the rehabilitative ideal.

Aside from these philosophical issues, it is also necessary to distinguish other approaches to crime and the penal system which may utilize the philosophical arguments but draw heavily on socio-political traditions. Briefly, there are three separate approaches, the rehabilitationists, the liberal reformist, and the radical non-interventionist.[21] Each provides a general framework but within that framework various sub-types operate. However, as we are concerned with generalities, the three approaches can be seen as ideal types. The rehabilitationist approach requires no further elaboration, so we can concentrate for the moment on the others. The liberal reformist position lies nearest to the rehabilitationist, whilst the radical non-interventionist is the most extreme and the most isolated. Consider first the liberal reform.

The liberal reformist position is in many ways an extension of the rehabilitation or treatment view, but instead of emphasizing individual pathologies it is more concerned with social class differences. Liberal reformists point to the overpresentation of convicted criminals from the lowest social classes, but they compare these results with studies of hidden delinquency which show that criminal acts occur within all social classes but the working classes appear to be singled out for punishment. The literature offering a liberal reformist perspective tends to suggest that working class criminals are a form of structural sacrifice. Denis Chapman could be regarded as a liberal reformist when he suggests that criminal behaviour is general but the incidence of conviction is controlled in part by chance and in part by social processes which divide society into the criminal and non-criminal, the former corresponding to roughly the poor and underprivileged. Chapman goes on to say:

> The designation and social isolation of a relatively small group of victims permit the guilt of others to be symbolically discharged: the identification of the criminal class and its social ostracism permit the reduction of social-class hostility by deflecting aggression that could otherwise be directed at those with status, power, reward, and property. A special part of [this] ideology functions to prevent the designated criminal from escaping from his sacrificial role, and institutional record keeping maintains his identity.[22]

Chapman not only identifies the relatively small group of convicted criminals which he calls victims, but draws attention to the relatively larger groups who break the law. He argues that one group, the 'victims', have the function of symbolically accepting society's criminal guilt. Without attempting to evaluate this argument the important point in Chapman's thesis is that he shifts the emphasis from individual offenders towards social class conflicts. In this way he regards the administration of justice as problematic and at the same time echoes some of the main streams of the liberal reformist position, i.e. that crime reduces social class hostility by deflecting attention.

The liberal reformists emphasize sociological theories such as anomie, subcultural theories, and those related to varying police activity as it operates to produce more working class criminals. Having stressed these points, liberal reformists then opt for piecemeal reform of society by introducing compensatory elements within the social structure. These reforms would be about wanting more assistance for working class criminals, i.e. more detached youth workers for potential delinquent groups, and a reduction of poverty within slums. Liberal reformists then re-emphasize that criminal acts occur throughout the social structure, not just amongst working class offenders. For example, they would draw attention to the motoring offender and the person who defrauds the income tax authorities as areas where police activity could be more usefully directed. In short, they would draw heavily on arguments about crime and the deprived social class, and their solutions would be to ease the deprivation.

The solutions within the penal system follow similar lines. Whilst not advocating abandonment of the courts' right to punish, they would none the less try to mitigate the punishment by a more humanistic philosophy. They would oppose a prison system which advocated more discipline and fewer personal privileges, and argue for an approach which reduced the numbers sent to prison because prison was not justified for that type of crime. They would also argue for more probation hostels, more hostels for ex-prisoners and an extension of the probation service. Liberal reformists would accept the need for treatment but their overall emphasis would be to see treatment as a means to an end, rather than an end in itself. Liberal reformists accept that there is some intrinsic value in treatment but only as long as it helped the offender to be more successful in manipulating his environment, and particularly with manipulating the economic environment.

Many rehabilitationists would share most of the assumptions of the liberal reformer, but the liberal reformer would probably criticize rehabilitationists for failing to give emphasis to a wider social perspective. On the other hand, both would welcome what they see as the increasing humanization of the penal system, and both in their various ways would emphasize the problems of the criminal rather than the victim.

Both groups have something else in common too. They each play down the role of law and play down the influence of power. Encapsulated as they are in their overriding concern with the criminal they create an unreal division between the criminal and crime, although the liberal reformer does of course emphasize the discrepancies in police practice. Both groups are in their way committed to piecemeal reform whether it be of the social system or of the penal system. However, it is worth emphasizing one difference, that whereas the liberal reformer offers a humanistic philosophy within his theoretical framework, humanism is not a necessary part of the treatment approach. It may exist within it but this is incidental; in its pure form treatment does not permit humanism except as a tool of rehabilitation, and that tool need not be included in any treatment plans.

The radical non-interventionist is philosophically isolated from the other two groups. Taking his main theoretical stance in radical sociology he is critical of all attempts at piecemeal reform, whether it be social or penal. If he has a coherent philosophy which could be neatly summarized it would be for radical social change outside the penal system and for a limited role of the courts within the penal system. On the other hand, some would still attempt to reduce the role of the courts without buying the rest of the package. Lemert, for example, in his analysis of the juvenile court, suggests that the juvenile courts should only be used as a last resort,[23] and not as advocated by the rehabilitationists as a treatment clinic, or by the liberal reformists as an institution where the juvenile can be provided with better social and economic opportunities.

Whilst the radical non-interventionist position is as yet unformulated — but incidentally no less so than any other penal philosophy — one area in which all radical non-interventionists agree is on the question of compulsory treatment. Sharing as I do some of the assumptions of the radical non-interventionists, it seems worth expanding this point before examining other features of rehabilitation.

Therapy, say Berger and Luckmann, entails the application of conceptual machinery to ensure that actual or potential deviants stay within the institutional definition of reality.[24] This requires a body of knowledge that includes a theory of deviance, a diagnostic apparatus, and a conceptual system for the curing of souls. Having acquired such a framework, therapists are then faced with an additional question of who do they do their therapy to. Central to the radical non-interventionists' position is the view that therapy within the penal system is enforced. By opposing such coercion they are echoing views of nineteenth century liberals such as John Stuart Mill who saw enforced therapy (not of course in those terms) as a violation of liberty. In a famous passage, Mill asserts that the only purpose for which power can be rightfully exercised over any member of a civilized community against his will is to prevent harm to others. His own good, either physical or moral, is not a sufficient warrant.[25] Mill, of course, was concerned with the actual procedure of arrest and incarceration, not about enforced therapy after incarceration, but the point about the individuals' own good is equally applicable. Mill's argument was also stated by the Gladstone Committee in 1895 when they thought it no business of the state to reform offenders. Neither would it appear to be any business of the state to be concerned with offenders' motives. The rule of law, to the Gladstone Committee, should be restricted to actions, and not include wishes, desires or thoughts.

Apart from opposing the coercive elements of rehabilitation, radical non-interventionists are also largely agreed that there should be more discussion about the issues involved in dispensing justice. Under the influence of the rehabilitative ideal, questions about justice have been ignored, and in some quarters seen as irrelevant. Where justice has been debated, it has usually been about individualized justice, and that is not necessarily the same thing. Issues about justice have become more prominent since the 1969 Children and Young Persons Act when the juvenile courts lost some of their power to the social services departments. The issues have only become clear when the social services acquired wide discretionary powers both before and after the court appearance and those powers are now wider than those of the juvenile courts before the Act was passed. In juvenile justice the expert has become pre-eminent, in this case the social services expert.

Most of the issues related to justice and enforced therapy are amplified in the area of juvenile justice, and it is no accident that the intensity of the debate about juvenile justice has produced the ideal types of treatment, liberal reform, and radical non-interventionists. With adults, there is a much less clear-cut pattern, but because it is more vague it has tended to obscure some of the finer points of those various models. To some extent this is due to the powers of judiciary, and particularly in the High Courts, who have resisted invasion of treatment experts into their traditional domain. In the juvenile courts magistrates have readily embraced the treatment model and have been more content to abdicate their position. Although radical non-interventionists are likely to focus most of their criticism on juvenile justice, they still have a great deal to say about the adult sphere.

The theory behind juvenile justice is based on the same assumptions that lie behind all treatment models; i.e. that bad equals mad — or to put it in current jargon, the depraved are really deprived. Juvenile offenders therefore are by definition wanting the experts' help, either because their offence was a 'cry for help', or because the offence was symptomatic of some deeper psycho-social problem. Now of course some children do need help but, having said that, it is a big step to assert that all delinquents need help, or that a theory of justice should be based on such a premise. However, the assumption behind the 1969 Act is that the depraved children are really only deprived. This means that there may be some who are depraved but are seen as deprived because the depraved and the deprived have the same basic problems. Sparks makes the point that such an assumption is unwarranted.

> It may well be true that a substantial proportion of both the depraved and the deprived have similarly unsatisfactory family or home backgrounds, equally limited educational attainment. The fact remains that — to put it simply — the one group steals and the other does not.[26]

The crucial difference is as Sparks says, not about family backgrounds but about attitudes, because the depraved, in contrast to the deprived, may have 'some distinctive attitudes towards property', and 'some very unfortunate attitudes towards authority'. Armed with the premise that delinquency is no different from other forms of antisocial behaviour, or rather it is a symptom of some deprivation, then the differences described by Sparks are likely to be glossed over.

Having adopted the stance of the radical non-interventionists, in as much as they are concerned with justice, this brief discourse into the alternative ideologies of rehabilitation, and liberal reform will, I hope, show that there are other ways of viewing the penal system apart from the reformist position. In this chapter there has been no attempt to provide an exhaustive account of alternatives, merely to open up the discussion before proceeding to a more detailed critique of one particular ideology. I am therefore concerned with social engineering because I share one major assumption of the radical non-interventionalists and that is their concern for justice. I would assert that such an emphasis is long overdue. Yet the components of justice must be a matter for continuous debate. Hopefully, the debate will be as wide as possible, taking in various aspects of the work of the courts, the composition of the courts, and will above all link the courts to the rule of law. I hope to show in the following chapters that the emphasis placed on the criminal's psycho-social background has stifled discussions about justice and placed important decisions in the hands of experts who have been more concerned with assessing, diagnosing and classifying deviants than about these social and political issues. David Matza equates justice with a sense of fairness, and if this is so, then the rehabilitative ideal is manifestly unjust by this definition.[27] In order to substantiate this assertion, we must first examine some of the assumptions behind the rehabilitative ideal and show how these assumptions are put into practice.

2

REHABILITATION, CRIME AND LAW

The essence of rehabilitation is that punishments should fit the criminal not the crime — or perhaps it would be more accurate to say that treatment should fit the criminal, for rehabilitationists eschew notions of punishment in the deterrent retributionist sense of that term. From this fundamental principle three major themes emerge which will appear and reappear throughout this book. First, that rehabilitation requires that professional judgments have to be made at certain key points in the rehabilitative process. This means that judgments will centre around basic questions of who is to be rehabilitated, who does the rehabilitation and what methods are to be used. It also raises the important question about whether rehabilitation can ever be regarded as complete. Most of these issues will dominate the middle chapters. In reply to the question of who is to be rehabilitated the answer for these purposes can be dealt with now. It is simply this: everyone who enters the penal system. In other words the decision to rehabilitate is decided by the administrators of justice rather than the reformist agencies them-selves. In this sense I am not concerned with those rather special areas of rehabilitation extending beyond the formal penal system such as the prevention of crime. Preventative measures are too important to be dealt with here for they pose their own special social and political problems which require a separate analysis. I am assuming that re-habilitation means being sentenced in order to be helped and this assumption demands an acceptance of a legally proven criminal offence. Again, I shall not be concerned with issues about whether the court was right to convict an offender, or whether an offender ought to have been acquitted at his trial, but like the rehabilitationists themselves I shall accept the court's findings as given.

The second major theme is concerned with the way supporters of rehabilitation posit a consensus model of society. This theme will be the subject matter of the last chapter on prisons, although it appears occasionally in this chapter and in other parts of this book, particularly in that section concerned with the experts. The third and final theme, that concerned with the emphasis placed on the criminal to the exclusion of crime and the criminal law, will be the major subject of this chapter. This too will reappear briefly in other parts of the book and particularly in the last chapter when some of the major implications of the rehabilitative model are discussed. Inevitably the themes will be dealt with on a wide conceptual basis; space does not permit a more exhaustive analysis, but hopefully some generalizations can be made which will be of value.

Before discussing the last of the three themes some more conceptual ground clearing is needed. I am making the assumption that the rehabilitative ideal is one basic model although in fact numerous models exist and rehabilitationists might disagree amongst themselves about the emphasis to be placed on each of these models. Sometimes rehabilitationists speak of individualized justice as the basic model, and by this I think they mean that the punishment/treatment should fit the criminal. Others use the medical model as their basic model and here it is not always clear if they mean an organic medical model or simply a model which uses the principles of diagnosis and treatment without being concerned with the physical basis of the disease. Some psychiatrists would use the organic medical model in their treatment of mental illness whilst others would operate within the principles of diagnostic/treatment models and claim they are treating a behavioural disease which they conceive as analogous to an organic disease. Social workers, particularly probation officers, use the latter model. It is often difficult to pick one's way through this conceptual confusion and to simplify the position I shall use the individualized justice model as being interchangeable with the diagnosis/treatment model. There are good empirical reasons for doing so; the Fabian Society for example uses both and uses them interchangeably in its memorandum to the Royal Commission on the Penal System. The Fabians thought that approved schools and borstals should be turned into genuine *treatment* centres where residents would receive *individual* attention and where treatment would be flexible.[1] Following the Fabian Society's example this means that when any other model is mentioned, such as the organic one, this will be stated, otherwise individual justice will mean the same as diagnosis and treatment.

The theme of this chapter then is concerned with the emphasis placed on the criminal to the exclusion of crime and the criminal law.

The chapter will be divided into three main sections. The first section will be concerned with the problematic nature of law, the second with the administration of justice and the third with the social pathology model.

We can begin the first section by noting that early criminological texts, and particularly those with a rehabilitative persuasion, rarely discussed crime, or if they did they did not incorporate it into their analysis. Sometimes it was assumed that crime had to be defined within the strict limits of the criminal law. If so, it was noted that laws change, and that changes in law made criminology a precarious scientific discipline, particularly when the subject matter was to be defined by lawyers. Having made these points — all of which incidentally are so obviously true — that part of the subject matter was seen to be completed. The rest of the book was concerned with criminals — and particularly with the epidemiological, psychological, and social aspects of their behaviour. Alternatively, crime was defined in non-legal terms, probably in the form suggested by Garofalo, i.e. as an act that offends the moral sentiments of pity and probity in the community. If so, there was no difficulty about moving to the next theme which was to discuss criminals.

Garofalo's definition is particularly interesting, for unlike the former example where crime is defined as a legal entity but never referred to again, Garofalo at least grasps the essential problem. As a scientific positivist he does not want to link the study of crime to the criminal law for this would demystify his scientific posture and reduce his scientific credibility. The solution was to define crime in behavioural terms. Yet by ignoring crime as a legal entity Garofalo is in fact offering a theory of behaviour and not a theory of crime.

Garofalo, and later supporters of rehabilitation, have been concerned with questions about why a particular person is a criminal. These explanations are usually made in terms of that person's psycho-social development, but this does not explain why he is a criminal. It only explains his behaviour. In other words theories of crime must offer two sets of explanations; first in terms of a theory of behaviour — presumably explaining why the person behaves as he does — but the second explanation must be in terms of why that particular person became labelled as criminal. Clarence Ray Jeffrey makes a similar point when he says that to ignore the legal status of crime is only to study deviant behaviour, and a study of deviant behaviour does not tell us why A is in prison and B is on probation.[2] Jeffrey, by implication, suggests that the problem shifts from questions about how and why an individual commits anti-social acts to questions about how the criminal law is administered. By extending Jeffrey's argument we can also include the prejudicial stage, and so take account of police activity, police decisions

to prosecute, and police discretions in law enforcement.[3] The suggestion
here is that crime has special features which extend over and above
other social rules, namely that crime includes certain types of behaviour
selected for specific formal sanctions.[4] These sanctions have to be
applied through a body of formal rules and formal decisions have to
be made about imposing these sanctions. Not all anti-social behaviour
qualifies for these sanctions, and not everyone who breaks these formal
rules is labelled as criminal. The criminal is the one to whom the label
has been successfully applied, and the application of that label requires
its own explanation.

Failure to appreciate that two sets of explanations are required has
led to a confusion in the literature and a lack of agreement about the
nature of crime. Whilst some criminologists such as Sutherland regard
crime as anti-social behaviour, and in doing so echo Garofalo, others
such as Tappan echo Beccaria and Bentham and see crime as a command
of the Sovereign backed up by sanctions. The extent of the confusion
is highlighted by Sutherland's study of White Collar Crime, which was
never really about White Collar Crime but about White Collar Criminals.
Had it been about crime Sutherland would have had to examine law and
societal reactions to that law, whereas he was only concerned about
people who had behaved anti-socially and about those who had learned
their deviant acts through differential association.[5]

Now Sutherland was not of course a supporter of rehabilitation but
he was a positivist and as we shall see later, rehabilitation uses the
positivist approach to provide the basic framework for its theory.
Positivists, concerned as they are with the scientific study of criminals,
have rarely considered that they are studying only one facet, that of
the person's deviant behaviour, and have not included in their analysis
any study of crime. Placing their trust in science, the only scientific
route available to them has been via the criminal, but unhappily for
the rehabilitationists there are no offenders without the implementation of the criminal law, and this they have chosen to ignore.

Rehabilitationists, then, unless they include in their theory the
application of the criminal label are not advancing a theory of crime.
Such an important defect in their theory has other implications which
need underlining. The first is that they do not regard crime and the
criminal law as problematic, but take it for granted, and it follows
from this that they do not regard the process of labelling as problematic
either. In some strange way the criminal is only seen as a person who
has behaved anti-socially and above all, who has problems. It is thought
to be enough to consider those problems as a means of providing a
theory about criminals. But crime is socially defined, and cannot for
that reason alone be taken for granted.

To say that crime is socially defined means two separate things.

First, it means that the criminal law changes, and what is a crime must change too. This point was almost always picked up by texts on rehabilitation, but then soon discarded, yet it was of such theoretical importance that one wonders how it could have been so neglected. Second and of more importance, crime is socially defined in the sense that crime is a product of certain types of societies. There was no crime in primitive societies because there was no criminal law. There may have been behaviour which offended key norms but this was not crime. If that behaviour was dealt with by the tribal elder, then it became 'behaviour dealt with by tribal elders' or some such other name, but it was still not crime. Crime can only be defined in terms of behaviour that offends the criminal law, and the criminal law as it now exists is a peculiar feature of modern industrial societies.

There is another sense too in which crime is socially defined, and that is that it involves a specific study of those who are prepared to break the law, *knowing their behaviour was a crime*. Ban, says David Matza, stops most people at the invitational edge, and if this is so, there are questions which must be asked about those who intentionally move over the invitational edge. This means that a phenomenological approach is needed to understand the full nature of the criminal act. Perhaps those who intentionally commit crime have a greater sense of excitement about breaking legal rules than those who are say unwilling victims. On the other hand some may not regard their behaviour as 'criminal' and laws may not hold their support. Furthermore others may not know they are committing criminal acts, whilst some may be wrongly labelled by the police and the courts. The offenders' psychosocial development becomes only one small part of a full theory of crime, yet it is on that small part that the rehabilitation position rests.

The problem for supporters of rehabilitation has always been one of deciding whether to incorporate crime within their study. Usually it is seen as a metaphysical concept and therefore to the scientist not worthy of inclusion. Alternatively, it can be seen as outmoded and outdated and equally unworthy of comment. It could also be reified and reification in this context means that crime and the criminal law are regarded as a formal embodiment of a society's ultimate values.

Rehabilitationists tend to opt for reification. In the examples given in chapter I criminals were seen as diseased, and Professor Flew gives the example of the psychiatrist who saw everyone who broke social rules as being in need of some form of psychiatric help. Yet by suggesting that everyone who breaks the law is diseased there is an implicit assumption that laws are a formal embodiment of social health. Laws then are not seen as the product of competing interest groups, nor of the arbitrary application of power, but represent a total configuration of what everyone knows 'ought to be'.

The very nature of law tends to support reification. Law is imperialistic and diverse, it also has an ability to freeze and codify social life. Lawyers also reify law so that at one point they appear to agree with rehabilitationists when they argue that law represents ultimate social values. Differences occur when rehabilitationists make that short but enticing step from the position where law represents ultimate values, to another position where law represents ultimate values of social health. The link between reification and social health is easily and deceptively made.

Essentially, by opting for reification rehabilitationists are further compounded to take the criminal law and the administration of justice for granted. Yet the criminal law is highly problematic and the first generalization that can be made about law is that few generalizations can actually be made. Paul Rock puts the point well:

> Just as social rules are varied in their structure and composition, so laws are anything but homogeneous. Few generalizations can usefully be made about the corporate body of laws. Laws differ in their intention and significance, their effects, their mode of development and the extent to which people acquire commitments to their perpetuation and enforcement.[6]

Apart from the diversity of law there is little else that can be said about it in any general sense. Neither is Rock hopeful that anything can be gained from analysing each law and attempting to generalize from the specific. Instead he thinks it is wise to distinguish between forms of law so that more internally consistent units are produced. The difficulty is of course to decide which forms of law require examination.

To give some illustrations of the problematic nature of law, consider the lawyer's own attempts to impose classifications. Whilst it is well known that the division between indictable and non-indictable offences can only be understood within the contractual nature of each offence, non-lawyers may be excused for assuming that some rudimentary classifications could be made, particularly about a fundamental principle of law such as 'mens rea'. But apparently not. Professor John Smith highlights the problem.

> The mental element in crime is technically known as *mens rea.* Though sometimes spoken of as 'the guilty mind' *mens rea* does not imply any feeling of guilt or of knowledge of wrong doing on the part of the person convicted. His ignorance of the criminal law is not a defence, so he may have *mens rea* though he believes his act is morally and legally right.[7]

21

Smith's point is that 'mens rea' can apply without a feeling of guilt or knowledge of the wrong doing. He illustrates this by the example of an immigrant who intends to take a second wife and has the 'mens rea' required for bigamy though he is unaware that English criminal law prohibits such conduct. On the other hand the immigrant would lack 'mens rea' if he reasonably believed that his first wife was dead or divorced or that his first marriage was a nullity.

The difference between 'mens rea' and strict liability offences adds a further complication. Smith again:

> In absolute offences or offences of strict liability the *mens rea* principle is not fully applied. A person is liable to conviction though he was unaware of one or more of the essential constituents of the crime. Thus a man took a girl who was under the age of 16 out of the possession of her father. That act was a statutory offence. He believed on reasonable grounds that the girl was 18. If she had been 18 the act would not have been an offence. He was found guilty.[8]

With strict liability offences, it does not matter if the defendant did not intend to do the act forbidden by law, or even that he was negligent. The mistake may be a reasonable one. Smith gives the example of a butcher prosecuted for selling defective meat when the butcher may have reasonably believed that the meat was fit to eat, and he could not have discovered otherwise except by employing an analyst. The butcher like the man with the 16 year old girl was still guilty.

The major source of confusion does not necessarily stem from the definitions of 'mens rea' or strict liability but from the legal interpretation of statutes. The criminal law is built up by case studies as well as by statutes and case studies often contain contradictory assertions about whether an offence is or is not one of strict liability. The Dangerous Drugs Acts, for example, were accepted as absolute offences from 1920 until the middle 1960s but suddenly in one celebrated decision (Sweet v. Parsley) the Court of Appeal ruled that they involved 'mens rea'. A reversal of all previous rulings needs its own separate analysis and in this particular instance the change in the social composition of the drug offenders appeared to be the crucial factor.[9]

The example given above highlights some of the major difficulties in attempting to analyse law by simply adopting the legal distinctions favoured by lawyers. Legal distinctions are rarely clear — even lawyers require qualifications at each level of analysis — so that Smith can define strict liability offences in terms of an absence of 'mens rea', but also defines them as existing where 'mens rea' is not fully applied. Where there are contradictions in case law and sudden reversals of previous judgments the non-lawyer finds himself in an analytically confusing area. Even so, the example given above of the Dangerous Drugs Acts shows that the social situation in which law is applied can never be ignored. A purely legal distinction operating in a social vacuum is of little help to the social scientist, and particularly the sociologist. William Chambliss's study of the laws of vagrancy showed that changing social conditions create a perceived need for legal changes and that these alterations will be effected through existing statutes. So in the case of vagrancy the laws were dormant from the sixteenth century until they needed to be revised and modified to take account of new patterns of industrialization.[10] Chambliss's study and the study of the Dangerous Drugs Acts demonstrate the validity of Hall's assertion that 'the functioning of the courts is significantly related to concomitant cultural needs and this applies to the law of procedure as well as substantive law'.

The problems involved in analysing law in terms of its content are simply that the whole body of law contains anomalies of interpretation, conflicting decisions and a mass of legal rules which may be dormant or used in ways entirely different to those for which they appeared to have been originally intended. Again the Dangerous Drugs Acts, for example, were originally concerned with stopping addiction in other countries. Heroin and cannabis were proscribed drugs because Britain wished to help the Chinese to suppress opium smoking and the Egyptians to suppress the use of hashish. That these Acts were used to control drug taking in Britain some forty years later could not have been foreseen. In a recent attempt to classify one branch of the offences of violence Hadden and McClintock concluded that there was little chance of making any sense of the mass of statutory offences except in terms of their legislative history.[11] They found they could not make a primary distinction between offences of violence based on the seriousness of the injury nor on the penalties provided. The emphasis on intent complicated this simple gradation. Murder, for example, is classified as the most serious crime in law but attempted murder is more serious than manslaughter which involves killing but without intent. Malicious wounding with intent is more serious in law than malicious wounding without intent, but infanticide which involves killing a child has a maximum penalty below that of malicious wounding.

If lawyers have been unable to make meaningful generalizations about law, have sociologists been more successful? Regrettably not, and the sociology of law has, until recently, made little conceptual advance since Durkheim and Weber. Durkheim has been the most frequently quoted sociologist in criminological circles, and perhaps the most frequently misunderstood. At one level he appears to be saying that law represents absolute values but at other times he seems to be shifting his position.[12]

Durkheim saw law as representing the principal forms of social solidarity which he thought grew out of the collective conscience.

> The common characteristic of all crimes is that they consist — except some apparent exceptions — in acts universally disapproved of by members of each society, i.e. crimes shock sentiments which for a given social system are found in all healthy consciences.[13]

Now in one sense Durkheim was right; crimes do shock common sentiments, or at least some crimes do. He was equally right when he asserted that

> We must not say an action shocks the common conscience because it is a crime, but rather that it is criminal because it shocks the common conscience. We do not reprove it because it is a crime, but it is a crime because we reprove it.[14]

The function of law — and Durkheim was discussing law, not anti-social behaviour — is in Durkheim's terms to defend the common conscience against all enemies from without and within. Law, to Durkheim, differed from other rules because it was applied in a formalized manner. But not all behaviour which shocks sentiments is a crime, not even all behaviour which shocks collective sentiments. What then distinguishes a crime? Durkheim saw the collective sentiments to which crime corresponds as being singularized by certain distinctive properties. First the behaviour must offend sentiments which are strongly engraved on all consciences, and second the sentiments must be precise. Crime then offends strong and defined states of the collective conscience — the collective conscience being defined as 'social likeness'.[15]

For our purposes, Durkheim's analysis points to certain important features of law which ostensibly support the view that law represents absolute standards of social health. Law develops from healthy consciences, and its function is to protect those consciences. Punishment has the 'true function of maintaining social cohesion intact by maintaining the common conscience in all its vitality'. Punishment to Durkheim is merely the 'double object' of law, for law prescribes certain obligations, as well as defining the sanctions attached to them. By suggesting that law is found in healthy consciences Durkheim is also suggesting that people who break the law do not have healthy consciences — which is another way of saying that law and law breakers provide indices of social health.

Yet Durkheim's analysis is defective for a number of reasons. First he argues that one of the distinctive features of law is that it shocks sentiments which are precise. But how can sentiments ever be precise?

They are by definition a loose amalgam of feelings. Second he saw law as offending sentiments which are strongly engraved on all consciences. Again some sentiments may be both precise and engraved on all consciences — adultery for example — which are not laws. And third, his analysis ignores the role of elite groups in law making and law enforcement. He attempted to deal with this difficulty by suggesting that certain groups have been authorized as the interpreters of collective sentiments.

> Power is wielded by a privileged class or by particular magistrates. But these facts do not lessen the demonstrative value of the proceedings, for simply because collective sentiments are enforced only through intermediaries it does not follow that they have ceased to be collective while localising themselves in a restricted number of consciences.[16]

It may not follow logically, but it certainly follows empirically, that the law makers and law enforcers are more likely to reflect the sentiments of what Troy Duster calls the 'moral centre'[17] than to reflect the sentiments of the other law abiding citizens. Yet it is precisely this feature of law as being related to elite groups and power, which presents the most serious obstacle to accepting Durkheim's view. Law may prescribe behaviour and prescribe punishment but the ability to pass laws depends on the ability to obtain powerful positions within society, and once in that position one need not legislate according to the collective consciences.

A closer look at Durkheim's analysis suggests that when he located law in the healthy consciences this did not mean that he wanted to 'treat' the unhealthy ones. What he wanted to do was heal the wounded consciences and this is not the same thing. In one sense he was more a supporter of retribution and deterrence than rehabilitation. A person offending the collective conscience would damage the collective consciences and they would need to be healed by an emotional reaction. Otherwise 'a slacking of social solidarity would ensue'. The method of healing was by 'an authentic act that can only consist in suffering inflicted on the agent'. The retributive position follows naturally. 'That is why it is right to say that the criminal must suffer in proportion to his crime, and only theories which deny that punishment has any expiatory character seem to so many people to be subservice of the social order.'[18]

Steven Lukes points out that behind this argument of Durkheim's was a rudimentary form of crowd control but Durkheim's view of punishment was curiously enough closely akin to the deterrent philosophy for he thought that 'punishment does not serve or only serves very secondarily to reform the guilty, it is intended above all to act upon honest persons since it serves to heal the wounds done to the collective sentiments'. Bentham argued in a similar vein, although for different reasons, when he justified punishment on the grounds of controlling the actions of those who had not committed a crime.

In an unexpected way Durkheim's arguments about law and social health lead him in the opposite direction to the rehabilitationists. Having reified law to the point where crime is seen as being able to shock collective sentiments Durkheim's analysis allows him to support a 'punitive' deterrent philosophy rather than a treatment one. Kai Erikson, in a similar vein, shows that law has the function of delineating boundaries and defining the outer edges of social space. 'People who gather together in communities need to be able to describe and anticipate those areas of experience which lie outside the immediate compass of the group — the unseen dangers which in any culture and in any age seem to threaten its security.'

The deviant himself is a visible reminder of violation of group norms, the net effect of deviant activity being to provide the necessary group solidarity. 'It may be that without the ongoing drama at the outer edges of group space the community would have no inner sense of identity and cohesion, no sense of the contract which sets it off as a special place in the larger world.' [19]

Seen in this way law is not there to provide a standard of absolute values but as a way of freezing or codifying social life. The overall effect may as Paul Rock says produce numerous sets of values, each absolute within a particular group. By adding 'concreteness' to illicit behaviour, by formally underlining it, control agents such as the police are entrusted to 'do their duty' and bring deviants to the courts. [20] The labelling process can then force the deviant into further deviant acts so that secondary deviation ensues. Both the control agents and the deviants are then provided with certain meanings about law and its enforcement in which both groups require a considerable stake. Cohesion is therefore produced in a number of different worlds; within the non-deviant group, amongst the deviants and amongst the law enforcers. Each group may at one level be functionally dependent on the other, but at another level be ideologically hostile. The overall effect is to produce a conflict which produces its own separate moral worlds, each world emphasizing certain values. Far from producing one absolute value, the delineation of social space provides numerous sets of values.

It is the functionalists who posit a benign social order with a minimum of conflict and it is mainly the functionalists who view law in terms of absolute values. Talcott Parsons sees law as acting as a means to resolve conflicts in an orderly way. [21] Conflicts are resolved through the courts by a willingness on behalf of members of the social system to use these courts. The courts are there to evaluate conflicts and their aims are based on the perceived goals of the social system as exemplified by the law. Harry Bredemeur[22] using a wholly functionalist approach sees the legal system as an integrative mechanism contributing to the overall co-ordination of the social system. First the political system itself provides the goals and powers of enforcement in exchange for the legal system to interpret the powers and legitimate them. Second, the adaptive system — i.e. science and technology in Western societies — provides knowledge and acceptance of queries as research directives in exchange for organizations and the demand for knowledge. Finally the pattern maintenance system, i.e. the method of bringing conflicts to the court's attention has the function of exchanging conflicts for resolution and justice. If the legal system is to be effective in contributing to integration, then these exchanges must be stable; if not, then dysfunctional features arise which upset the effectiveness of the legal system.

The functionalist approach has the great merit of highlighting particularly features of the consensus model of society; a model well summarized by Richard White.

> The consensus model views society as basically unitary. Parliament represents us all; the executive acts in the common interest . . . the law is equal and just to all and is administered without fear or favour for the common good . . . . Conflicts that there are will be on a personal level.
>
> The archetypal conflict will be the matrimonial problem, seen as a problem between individuals at variance with one another. Structural conflicts between interest groups if not entirely absent will be transformed into questions about the enforcement of individual obligations.[23]

The difficulty with the consensus model is that it is benign, and it is defective for that reason. Law is simply not something that applies equally and justly to all. Two people in court are not on an equal footing; the evidence of police invariably carries more weight than the defendants. In civil law the wealthy have a built-in advantage even before the case is heard. The wealthy can afford the better barristers and dare risk a greater loss in court costs. Paradoxically it is only the very poor on legal aid who can take such a risk. Furthermore, translating structural conflicts into personal ones simply ignores the structure. The myth of equality before the law is of course functional in itself so the argument becomes circular, but functionalists are also descriptively accurate when they assert that the individual should be postulated or viewed as existing not *against* the state but *within* the social system.

The other difficulty with the functionalist view is that it assumes that the presence of a rule or legal norm does little more than specify proper conduct. Yet legal norms are essentially two-sided, proscribing and prescribing behaviour so that in effect they delineate two groups, those who obey and those who do not. Delineations supported by denunciations of one group by another (in the court procedure they are defined by Garfinkel as successful degradation ceremonies) are not the most effective methods of producing total solidarity. The functionalists are able to ignore structural conflict because so little of their analysis is concerned with dysfunctions; more with latent functions. Having posited a benign social system, dysfunctions by definition are reduced to a minimum, so it is more convenient to regard *law breakers* as dysfunctional rather than the *law itself.*

But it is the absence of the consideration of power which is so defective in the functionalist analysis. The conflict model of law is equally persuasive. Dicey shows how it affects law when he says 'Men legislate not in accordance with their opinion as to what is good law, but in accordance with their interest.'[24] The conflict model is also clearly stated by White.

> [Society] consists of two sides, those who have power, authority or wealth and those who do not. Conflict is of a sacred or elemental type between two fundamental groups so that individuals and smaller groups have their position defined by the structure of the conflict and are forced into a situation where they can only exist as components in one or other of the two sides . . . . In this type of society law is the means by which the dominant group maintains its domination and enforces its will so that law is merely a mask behind which power is exercised.[25]

There are numerous defects in this model not the least being that society is a good deal more complicated than consisting simply of two sides — those with power, authority and wealth and those without it. The issue however, is not to debate alternative models but to show how the consensus model is defective. Certainly some laws are more appropriately viewed in terms of a conflict model but others, such as murder and violence, are conflict situations which can be viewed inside a consensus framework. Yet structural conflicts do exist, although to recognize some elements of a model is not to suggest that that model is the only one available. In this sense both the conflict *and* consensus are defective. The alternative is an open model which recognizes a continuing conflict of interests but as White says, sees these conflicts as being many-sided. The essence of this model is that individuals may find themselves playing different roles in different conflicts but these conflicts will be resolved within an established framework. That framework may change but not to the point where overt continuous conflict is advocated. Or as White says, 'In this sort of society it is accepted that there will be group conflicts but they will be contained within an element of consensus.'[26]

In the open model law has a more dynamic part to play, as well as being seen in terms of the overall body of rights. In the conflict model rights are discounted and in the consensus model they are meaningless. An open model also recognizes that law can represent powerful elitist groups, sometimes operating at the expense of others, sometimes acting to produce a system similar to that portrayed by the functionalists.

Once an open model is accepted — or at least once a model is accepted which incorporates some degree of conflict — we can think in terms of different networks and different moral worlds reinforced by the presence of law because law both divides and unifies. Paul Rock sees these moral worlds as having their own organizations of role beliefs and loyalties each in a somewhat differentiated form from its neighbour. The boundaries between them shape communication channels so that information and perspectives are unevenly distributed throughout the networks.[27] Each moral world is a potential and actual source of conflict, and deviancy, as Rock says, must be constantly neutralized if stable and uneventful relations between social worlds are possible. Law is that division and neutralizing agent. In this sense law is imperialistic because it encompasses all social worlds. It is the only institution of this type which has an overall legitimacy; other agents of control must be restricted to certain segments.

There is a good deal of evidence to support Rock's view of society having stratified systems in different moral worlds. For although law is imperialistic — and imperialism suggests a domination of one group over another — different laws acquire different meanings and different degrees of support in each moral world. Some laws, like recent legislation on abortion, homosexuality and capital punishment, are expressions of an elite group, and opponents become outsiders. Other laws, such as those on race relations and drug offences, may be expressions of a wider number of moral worlds representing both an elitist segment as well as non-elitist groups. Supporters of new laws on race relations for example could also find themselves outsiders in respect to the abortion laws. Moral worlds are not socially fixed or immutable but change according to the diversity of the laws. Viewed in this way law not only produces a diversity of values but separates groups into various moral worlds.

Recent studies show that there does not appear to be a great deal of consensus about law, whether it be about those who pass the laws or about which types of behaviour are or even should be controlled by law. In a survey of the literature in this area Berl Kutchinsky points to a study in 1964 by Walker and Argyle who surveyed knowledge about the Suicide Act of 1961. Apparently, a year after that Act had been passed only 16 per cent of the sample knew that suicide was no longer a crime, and no less than 75 per cent thought that attempted suicide was still a criminal offence.[28] More interesting for our purposes are the studies which examine the attitudes towards particular types of behaviour. Results in one study by Van Houtte and Vinke suggest that 'a general sense of justice does not exist'.[29] Reactions to legal rules differed widely and in some cases there was no majority opinion even about such behaviour as rape. Only 30 of the 52 legal rules listed in one investigation were accepted by more than 50 per cent of the respondents, and these rules were not ones which were peripheral to the main body of law. The author concluded:

> Many scholars of law and sociology who discuss the acceptance of rules of law maintain such concepts as 'moral judgment', 'social pressure' and 'law' as a totality. The present results make it more than clear that the attitudes towards various types of rules of law diverge widely. The hypotheses on which the survey was based are verified. Only the rules pertaining to neglect of important duties were universally accepted. Rules in the field of moral judgment, however, much rooted in tradition, no longer enjoy general social adhesion.[30]

These studies raise other questions. For example, why do, or why should people obey the law when they rarely agree about the content. The answer in one sense is plain enough: people simply do not obey, as over 2 per cent of the population of England and Wales appear in court each year. This answer if taken at its face value is misleading for it is possible to agree about the value of a law and still break it. Prisoners as a group tend to be politically conservative and rarely advocate changes in social legal rules outside the prison.[31] They are, in Joseph Gusfield's phrase, the cynical deviants, self seeking, rather than politically and morally motivated toward public welfare.[32] That people are able to contravene their beliefs so regularly is a question not confined to the sociology of law but is a key issue in moral philosophy and theology, and it is a question that can be examined empirically by studying every motorist when he takes his car on the road. These research studies, however, force us to reassess earlier conceptions of law, particularly those which saw law as built up on strong public sentiments. Sumner, for example, thought that legislation had to seek a 'standing ground' on the existing mores; Aubert in his covariance theory posited a necessary agreement between legal rules and legal behaviour. Bertrand Russell also asserted that 'law is almost helpless if it is not supported by public sentiment'.[33] Clearly the position is more complicated than that because as Van Houtte and Vinke show, attitudes about law vary widely. For example, one group may have a legalistic acceptance of rules which lead to a generalized view about law. They think law ought to be obeyed for the general welfare so that whilst individual offences may not be regarded as morally wrong certain types of behaviour should be proscribed if only because too much law breaking would dislocate society. Other groups may accept illegal behaviour, i.e. they advocate disapproval but do want punishment. Others may completely reject law, i.e no disapproval and no punishment. What is not known is whether those who completely rejected the law were more likely to break it. Possibly not, for the authors show that knowledge and opinion about law had few secondary effects. To know more about it did not alter behaviour very much. Lawyers and prisoners were no more law abiding than others.

The absence of any general consensus about legal norms is not a new finding but one that rehabilitationists have chosen to ignore. Subcultures, delinquent or otherwise, have been recognized by sociologists for a number of years. Rehabilitationists may also have recognized them too, but in doing so have tended to translate subcultural values into a form of defective socialization. Yablonsky, for example, writing about American groups in the slums called the gang members 'sociopaths' and stressed the formation of delinquent values as part of the disunited family system. A British psychiatrist (M. Glatt) writing about drug addicts in Piccadilly Circus misquotes Albert Cohen, or at least misunderstands him, by calling the addicts round Piccadilly Circus 'a drug subculture' and then sees the formation of the subculture as being related to 'a common problem of adjustment'. But whereas Cohen saw delinquent subcultures as stemming from a reaction to middle class value systems, Dr Glatt assumed that drug takers are *maladjusted* and their 'drug subculture' is a collection of maladjusted people. There does not seem very much point in attempting a vigorous defence of subcultural theories — the defects are too well known — but it is conceivable that groups exist in our society which simply do not have the middle class normative systems. They may have other values, but to call these group members 'maladjusted' shows a form of intolerance and lack of respect of people's right to be different.[34] Moreover Walter Miller has convincingly shown that working class groups have value systems which automatically lead to conflict with the law. Punishment may only reaffirm the member's position within his peer group, giving perhaps higher status than before. The example of Sikhs refusing to wear crash helmets may certainly be seen as a form of maladjustment, but only maladjustment to non-Sikh values.

A refusal to incorporate law into their discussion has led rehabilitationists to accept *the operation of the legal system* as a given entity, and not as a problematic one. Rehabilitationists operate only at the point where the penal system begins, i.e. when the person has been found guilty of the offence. Politically of course they are right to do so; it is not their business to become involved in the workings of the law. Yet not to be involved in the legal operation is quite different from ignoring these operations within their theoretical framework, and somehow assumes that the legal system will automatically provide offenders who are 'criminal'. Having considered law as problematic the legal circumstances under which a person came to appear before the court is part of the process which shows whether he is a criminal. To ignore it is again to revert to a theory of behaviour.

We come now to the second part of that process which is to consider the administration of justice as problematic. We can begin by using Weber's analysis of stages of law. Max Weber's analysis of the development of law and procedure at first points to a monolithic structure, but this is deceptive. Weber saw law as passing through several stages of development from what he calls 'the charismatic legal revelation through the law prophets' to the most advanced stage of 'systematic elaboration of law and professionalised administration of justice by persons who have received their legal training in a learned and formally logical manner'.[35] Some element of progression is inherent in Weber's work, for law appears to develop from the legal irrationality of Kadi justice found in the Moslem market place to the formal rationality of advanced legal systems. Weber, however, showed that elements of earlier systems are found amongst formally rational systems, where the bureaucratized judge is instructed by the legislators to arrive at his decision by 'individualizing' the case rather than relying on formal rules. Occasionally, judges in formally rational systems resemble the Kadi justice of the Moslems.

But Weber's 'stages' of law are not stages of 'truth', they are merely stages of procedure based on the level of bureaucratization. He was careful to show that bureaucratic administrators were not part of what he called 'an enormous vending machine' and that bureaucratization did not stultify the creativity of the official, rather it encouraged it, albeit with a limited framework. Formal rationality did not mean an absence of initiation but an absence of free discretion and *personally* motivated favour and evaluation. It also meant a supremacy of impersonal ends, and rational consideration.[36] So careful was he to distinguish between procedural norms and absolute truth that he said in one illuminating passage,

> It is perfectly clear that 'objectivity' and 'professionalisation' are
> not necessarily identical with the supremacy of general abstract
> rules not even in modern adjudication . . . . There have been violent
> objections against the conception of the modern judge as a vending
> machine into which the pleadings are inserted, together with the
> fee which then disgorges the judgments, together with its reasons
> mechanically derived from the Code.[37]

Weber did not see the judge as part of what he called a 'gapless
system of laws' but someone with relative freedom to operate and make
decisions within a formal framework. By this argument he suggested
that law was essentially a normative discipline rather than a mathemati-
cally and statistically orientated dispensary. By showing that there was,
and still is, resistance to the 'vending machine' type of justice he forged
links between sociology and the 'legal realists' school of law. The legal
realists, founded and influenced by Karl Llewellyn and Jerome Frank,
concentrated on the way in which judges and magistrates *made the law
rather than found it'*. They adopted a sceptical position toward all
judicial procedures. They were important because they directed
attention away from generalizations about types of authority and concentrated on the operation and interpretations within the law. They
insisted that all decisions by legal officials are made by 'one essentially
subjective grasp of the entire situation' and then rationality is added by
pinning the subjective element to legal doctrine. Justice Holmes, a
supporter of the legal realists, once remarked, 'You can give any conclusion a logical form.'[38]
    The legal realists questioned the whole of the courtroom procedure.
Their views are best summed up by Justice Holmes's famous comment
'that law is not a brooding omnipresence in the sky...'. This view
accepts the human qualities in decision making and rejects arguments
that there is some abstract objective truth which emerges in courts.
Law is essentially based on interpretation. The judge always has to
choose because he has to decide which principle will prevail and which
party will win, and the judge presumably decides according to a host of
variables such as his interpretation of justice, his experiences and his
own theoretical position about law. The judge has to decide whether
to quote a precedent, even before he decides which precedent he will
quote, and it is his decision to sum up the case in a particular way, to
decide which evidence to select, and which evidence to ascribe meanings
to. The courtroom itself then becomes an interplay of sociological as
well as legal forces. It is only the legal empiricists who see it as a place
where 'facts' emerge. Juries too have to decide,[39] and the recent

criticisms of their verdicts by Sir Robert Mark suggest that their negotiation of reality differs considerably from that of the police.[40]

Now there are of course limits to the legal realism argument. An extremist position would be held by those who see justice as 'gastronomic justice', i.e. decisions being made according to what the judge had for breakfast! Critics of the legal realists seriously used this argument as did some legal realists themselves. However, in its less strong form there is obviously much in legal realism, particularly for sociologists who have always concerned themselves with the social situation of the court and the processes which lead people to be labelled as criminal. Included under this heading would be the selection of certain legal statutes selected by the police as applicable for each case. Nigel Walker illustrates some of the problematic features involved in any police prosecution. He uses an example of domestic violence.

> A domestic brawl in which a husband hits the wife with a hammer could be classified under a number of [legal] headings. The choice of heading would be made by the police after their initial enquiries . . .
> . . . the classification would therefore be determined by the judgment and policy of the police and the more or less accidental features of the crime.
> Thus the husband who could be proved to have said before hitting his wife 'I am going to kill you' might well be recorded as an attempted murder; if he kept his mouth shut or if his words went unheard he would probably not. If the blow fractured her skull it would probably be recorded as a felonious wounding or even a mere indictable assault. If she successfully dodged it it might well be treated as a non-indictable assault. *Moreover from the clinical point of view it is fallacious to distinguish even murder from crimes of this sort since it is mere accident that determines whether an attempted murder succeeds or whether a blow that was merely intended to inflict harm has fatal results.* [41] (Emphasis mine.)

Walker's last point, concerning clinical distinctions, will be picked up later; at this stage it is only necessary to establish that the police 'as the first level of informers' have considerable influence over the whole decision making process. They influence the trial itself by their choice of legal statute under which they prosecute; they influence the type of court, since certain offences can only be tried in certain courts, and they also influence the sentence through the statute and the powers of the trial. The criminal label eventually applied is a product of a host of variables which includes the police, and as in Walker's example, includes witnesses too.

At a purely formal level any analysis of law which would include case law as well as statute law, and any analysis of the administration of justice must consider the developments and effects of each law. It must also include the extent to which people acquire commitments to the perpetuation and enforcement of those laws. Discrepancies, if and when they exist, provide further evidence for the analysis. Yet the very contradictions and diversities of law and legal norms leads to the conclusion that any theory of criminals must of necessity include a study of law. Leslie Wilkins saw crime as being something the police 'ought to do something about' and what they actually do is to become involved in making various decisions. A sequential model would show each decision and also show that at each stage the person who had acted anti-socially could drop out of the system. The model would show the first stage, where someone does something that the police ought to do something about, and finish at the offender's entry into the penal system. To omit these stages leaves a serious gap in any theory of crime.

The discussion on functionalism and the consensus model is not only relevant to a sociology of law but it shows where the rehabilitationists have traditionally and historically positioned themselves on the sociological network. This is not to say that rehabilitationists are functionalists but it is worth noting that functionalism and rehabilitation both had similar footholds in sociological theories of social disorganization. Similarly functionalism and rehabilitation both posit a benign social system each in their way supporting a particular type of consensus where deviants are located at points of structural strain. The arguments about 'problem families' in the 1950s showed how close the functionalists were to the rehabilitationists. Both saw problem families as exhibiting abnormalities within the social system: the functionalists saw them as being deviant within the main structure and the rehabilitationists conveniently provided the vehicle for their return to 'normality'. Whilst not actually using the same theoretical stance there was a certain harmony about their operations. Their goals were similar, the terminology was similar and both viewed the structure as benign.

This is now a convenient point to introduce the third and last theme of this chapter — the social pathology model. Social pathology has long dominated the rehabilitationist arguments, having certain features which are immediately appealing. It is individually based, it draws heavily on the methods of medicine and in doing so achieves unearned status, and it is appealing because it is orientated to individual change. It is defective for two main reasons, first because it fails to consider a wider social context and second because a social disease cannot be identified in the same way as a physical disease.[42]

The social pathology perspective has a long philosophical history, drawing as it does from natural law and from early sociological theories of Spencer and Durkheim. These sociologists used the 'organic analogy' where society was seen as an organism with individual human beings likened to a biological cell. John Rex has criticized the use of this analogy in sociology on the grounds that in healthy organisms the activities of the units and organs are almost entirely confined to those which have the effect of maintaining the life of the organism. With social organisms things are different, for people do things involving the co-operation of other people which do not have the effect of maintaining the social structure.[43] Further, as Rex says, in the case of biological organisms there is only one sort of explanation of an activity possible, and that is that biological organisms are explained when we have shown that they have the effect of maintaining the structure. Social activities are more complex, and the primary activities of human beings may not have any role to play in the maintenance of the social structure.

The organic analogy, however, is only a by-product, for the organic analogy and social pathology are not one and the same thing. Sociologists such as Durkheim who used the organic analogy were concerned to use it as a model for explaining society. Social pathologists on the other hand may use this model but the emphasis shifts as their arguments are individually based and are primarily concerned with identifying social disease or social sickness within society. The distinction is slight but crucial, for Durkheim was not a social pathologist, although he used the organic analogy.

Pathology refers to the study of the causes and nature of diseases and to unhealthy conditions and processes caused by disease. Social pathology then by definition, refers to the study of the causes and nature of social disease. Historically, social pathology has its roots in the ancient philosophical duality of the individual man versus society; harmony arises when the individual and society are in tune. Sometimes disharmony is created by the individual who upsets or disturbs society, sometimes it is society that is seen to be at fault. The emphasis changes and in the last thirty or forty years the individual has been seen as pathological but more recently the society has been singled out for attention. Although the emphasis may change, the basic solution remains the same, and that solution is always to be found in the health of the individual members.

In the early twentieth century when individuals were seen as pathological the solutions were first sought in terms of the biological and genetic origins of the diseased. Darwin's influence was here, so that people who were poor, criminal, or uneducated were regarded as genetically and biologically inferior. They represented the atavistic types who were unable to fit into the new progressive scientific society. Lombroso's search for the born criminal and other contemporary work on cretinism reflected this view. The recent interest in the XYY chromosome suggests that Lombroso's influence is still with us. Solutions to genetic and biological defects were occasionally sought in a eugenics policy which still reappears in various guises, such as when sterilization is advocated for mental defectives and castration is given to sex offenders in Holland.

After Lombroso's methods and techniques became discredited — mainly by one man, Charles Goring — emphasis shifted from the genetic to the emotional. The shift was a relatively easy one. By the early twentieth century Freud's theories were beginning to be known and it was not difficult to substitute the biological inferiority of the geneticists with the emotional inferiority of the Freudians. The emotional argument is still popular, relating neuroses and psychoses to the early patterns of family relationships. Both the biological and the emotional theories share a common view; that the present evil, be it crime, poverty or neuroses, can be traced to a past evil such as a biochemical disorder, brain damage, or defective relationships in the early years. The evil-begets-evil fallacy, as Kingsley Davis calls it, has long dominated thinking about the aetiology of crime.

Solutions have been sought in attempts to restore the patient to health. Under the biological/genetic school this could involve surgery, e.g. pre-frontal leucotomies. When the emphasis shifted to the emotional arena, the solutions were sought in terms of therapy. Surgery and therapy both attempt to remove those diseased parts of the patient in order that new healthy growth could be achieved. These two solutions, however, are not discrete alternatives and it is not a question of having surgery or therapy. It is possible to have both since the emotional argument still permits the possibility of hereditary defects. Solutions are in that sense transferable. With the changing emphasis away from the individual to society the emphasis shifts but the methods remain similar.

Rehabilitationists find the social pathology doctrine powerful and appealing. Their emphasis as far as the penal system is concerned can be firmly placed on the sick individual particularly as he has offended against the absolute values of society as expressed by the law. The difficulty is that someone must decide about what constitutes this social sickness and it is at this stage that conflict occurs. To examine this point — which incidentally is a constant and recurring theme throughout this book — a brief excursion is needed in the realm of physical medicine. Social pathologists, whilst drawing heavily on the organic analogy, also include the medical model of diagnosis and treatment to operationalize their concept.

Some critics of the social pathology perspective suggest that the analogy of society as an organism is misleading because physical health is value free whereas social life is not. They would stress bodily malfunctioning as a basic component of physical disease, yet Professor Flew is surely right when he says that physical diseases also have a strong normative component. At one level physical disease may be defined in neutral terms, i.e. as being related to the proper functioning of the organism, but ultimately terms like 'functioning' cannot be divorced from a cultural context. To be more precise, 'functioning' must be related to social roles within a given social universe. The example given by Flew will show what he means: A Trappist monk vows never to speak again, but are his vocal organs not functioning properly? Not by his standards nor by his definitions as they are functioning as he wants them to function. They would only be mal-functioning if he breaks his vows, tries to talk again and finds he cannot.

Diseases then, according to Flew, are very much culture bound, and to attempt to avoid the cultural element by suggesting there exists an absolute standard of health which can be medically determined surely misses the point. Diseases must invoke a subjective element being defined by the sufferer as bad for him, and recognized by him and his own values as being a bad thing. This is not to dismiss the bodily functioning argument, merely to add an important component.

The role of the doctor is of course the crucial element here. Consider what happens if the patient says he is diseased, and the doctor disagrees? Most likely the patient accepts the doctor's definitions because the doctor and patient are sufficiently in agreement about the norms surrounding the doctor's role. The relationship works well because we believe that the doctor's definitions fit our own, and they are pre-sumptively good for us. Where disagreements exist they are likely to be personalized, so that medical directives would not be accepted because the doctor was seen as being, say, sadistic or inefficient. Alternatively there may be disagreements at an ideological level as with Christian Scientists who may recognize that doctors have their best interests at heart, but would choose not to receive medical attention. (Even so they may still recognize that they are diseased.) It could of course be suggested that definitions about what is good for us are made by the doctor who defines them in his own terms, whilst the patient meekly accepts those definitions. Yet acceptance exists only because the medical profession has frequently demonstrated that the doctors' work has been largely in the patients' interests, and we believe that the medical profession operates in a way that is presumptively good for us.

To return now to the main social pathology argument: it is clear that the role of the social doctor is quite different from that of the medical doctor if only because there are few levels of agreement about what constitutes social sickness. Nor is it possible to expect that the designators of social sickness are always acting in a situation where they can say that a particular social sickness is a bad thing and is also

presumptively bad for us. What is good and what is bad in the wider
social arena is a matter for political, religious and social dispute the
world over. Of crucial importance is the point that social pathologists,
unlike the medical doctor, do not require the patient's agreement that
a social sickness is bad for them. Or to put it another way, a social
sickness does not have to have the patient's agreement. Without a basic
working definition of social health, social pathologists are in a rather
peculiar position of having to rely on their own definitions which may
or may not be acceptable to anyone else, least of all to the patient.
This is what Matza means when he says that rehabilitation produces a
system of 'rampant discretions', since a reliance of individual judgments means that judgments may differ and be out of tune with others.

Furthermore, within the social pathology perspective there are
disguised moral implications which show themselves in the individual
judgments of the social pathologists, particularly in the language they
use. 'Depersonalization', 'growth' and 'social awareness', all favourite
words of social pathologists, have strong moral overtones. The term
'growth' for example implies change, but the direction of that change
can never be a matter of moral indifference. In a curious way, 'growth'
may refer to individual growth, but this does not necessarily imply
consideration for the growth of others. Neither does it recognize that
growth means anything other than the efficiency of human relations.
Questions about the norms which have restricted growth are seldom
asked, or if they are, it becomes relatively easy to refer the whole matter
to biological or early emotional experiences. C. Wright Mills calls
this 'a paste-pot eclectic psychology' which he says 'provides a rationale
for a facile analysis'.[44] By transplanting the medical-patient roles to the
social arena the welfare of the individual patient becomes paramount.
In physical medicine there is rarely conflict about such a moral stance.
Most of the patient's contemporaries hope that the patient returns to
physical health, and a change from disease to health is likely to meet
with general approval. But growth, or a return to health in the social
pathological sense, may not meet such general approval since the
direction of that change is likely to be a matter for wider political and
social considerations. Two examples will clarify this point, the first is
an extreme case, the second more usual.

A probation officer has a man on probation who is diagnosed as
inadequate and inhibited. In line with that theoretical stance, the
probation officer regards a release of inhibitions as a form of growth.
Conceivably the probation officer will view a further crime, perhaps
an assault, as a form of growth but in doing so will ignore the moral
implications of this action, and particularly the implications for the
victim. (Probation officers have said in court that they have
welcomed a new offence as indicative of a change to social health.)

Alternatively, consider an example where relationships between married partners may have deteriorated. The psychiatric counsellor may advise a particular course of action — to commit adultery for example — which would have certain effects on the other partner if it were discovered. Such an insulated view of the patient as someone who operates in situations rather than in a wider social nexus is typical of the myopia inherent in social pathological thinking.

Such a reductionist position is two-sided. In the above example the effect of the patient's actions on others appeared to be ignored in the search for individual growth. The result is a one-sided encapsulation of the individual whose personality is seen to be formed early in childhood and who thereafter acts out these defects on the social stage in a way in which the social stage is largely irrelevant. No consideration appears to be given to 'the problem of the relations of men to one another'. C.A. Ellwood views social problems as a genuine interaction of social relationships.

> It is the problem of human living together, and cannot be confined
> to any statement in economic eugenic or other one-sided terms...
> it is as broad as humanity and human nature . . . Such a statement
> (in terms of one set of factors) obscures the real nature of the
> problem and may lead to dangerous one-sided attempts at its
> solution.[45]

Ellwood has little time for the 'one-sided approach' and would not be prepared to consider criminals as simply having deep-seated personal problems which can be removed as a result of some therapeutic relationship. Crime and criminals pose wider problems of analysis than that of the criminal's psyche or social background. Yet the one-sidedness is inherent in the rehabilitationist's position, adopting as they do the view that knowledge of individual crime is sufficient to produce solutions to the problems of crime. Crime is, however, socially defined whether it be in terms of the laws, the operation of the legal system, or the interaction between the criminal and his social world. The defect of the rehabilitationist argument lies in their refusal to incorporate these problematic areas into their view of deviance. Rehabilitationists are not therefore concerned with producing a full social theory of deviance, but as was said earlier, they are concerned with producing a theory of anti-social behaviour.

The one-sidedness has additional repercussions. Once the criminal's psyche and background are seen as the sole determinants in crime, a lack of attention is given to the other factors. Studies of the processes within the administration of justice are ignored, so is the role of the victim, as are the laws themselves. Rehabilitation has had a stultifying effect on criminology simply because it has refused to regard any other area as problematic. A sense of isolation has been produced, where studies of prisons have been about prisoners, studies of probation have been about the people on probation, and studies of mental hospitals have been about mental patients. Recently there have been attempts to remedy this by a small group of sociologists deriving their impetus from American theorists such as Becker, Lemert and Matza. Yet British criminology remains firmly anchored to the correctional perspective, isolated from other subjects except those directly concerned with scientific research methods, dynamic psychology, and positivist sociology. Lemert, adopting an extreme position, makes the point that rehabilitation has produced a scientific tyranny with power given to the research workers and practitioners which is little short of the Divine Right of Kings. The emphasis here needs to be on the word *'tyranny'* for that is exactly what Lemert meant. Hopefully this has begun to change if only because tyranny, like disease, is presumptively bad for *all* of us.

3

The experts

In this chapter I want to extend some of the points made earlier and pay particular attention to that aspect of social pathology which produced the experts. By experts I mean that group of people who claim to have special knowledge and skills and who 'diagnose' and 'treat' the offender's psycho-social worlds. Professor Flew calls them the 'soul doctors' but in less abrasive terms they are usually called psychiatrists, social workers and probation officers.

The relationship between the experts and the penal system is often complex, sometimes conflicting, and occasionally functionally interdependent. At one level experts accept the criminal law as capable of delineating boundaries between social health and disease. They also support the legal and penal institutions in which they operate, deriving status and power from their quasi-legal role. Yet paradoxically, as was shown in chapter 2, they also regard the criminal law as a crude and blunt instrument to use in any diagnosis, regarding it as metaphysical while they locate the social disease in the individual offender. They claim to operate at a more scientific level than lawyers and have a body of knowledge which equips them for their expert role. Sometimes they appear to resent the method of cross-examination in the courts, seeing it as socially demeaning for someone with their expertise to be subject to aggressive questioning and prefer to deal in more global terms than is permitted by the rules of evidence and the cross-examinatory procedure.

Experts, however, are not usually radicals or revolutionaries; their aim is person-change rather than social change, and gradual people-change at that. They may be concerned with increasing their power and influence but rarely wish to overthrow the existing legal order. More likely they want to fashion it in their image, an image which if past experience is anything to go by, means more power for them.

Experts are not new — they did not suddenly arrive with the timely growth of rehabilitation but developed from the neo-classical school of the eighteenth century. [1] The school is important for two reasons; first because it introduced the experts into the courts and second because neo-classicism is still the model used by the courts in Britain, and incidentally in all industrial societies throughout the western and eastern world.

The earlier classical school, under the influence of the utilitarians, saw man as a rational entity who, before committing an offence, weighed up the expected advantages with the expected punishments. Classicists concentrated solely on the criminal act. Individual differences between offenders could be ignored because man's rationality was seen as the beginning and end of the discussion. The eighteenth century man would be expected to have considered rationally the advantages and disadvantages of committing a criminal act and this would therefore require a system which adjusted punishments based on a simple method of deterrence. If people rationally decided that the advantages of committing a crime outweighed the disadvantages then the solution was clear — the punishment should be increased until the disadvantages became too great.

The difficulty which the classicists soon had to face was that their assumptions about rationality began to be questioned. People seemed to have differing degrees of rationality, and these seemed to be dependent on backgrounds and personality. In other words, some offenders appeared to be more rational than others. Rigid adherence to classicist principles meant ignoring obvious social and psychological differences which were thought to affect that degree of rationality. Once such criticisms began to be widespread, classicism was impossible to operate in its pure form.

The neo-classicists, who were the ardent critics of the classical school, modified classical principles but only at the stage where the punishment would be imposed. They did not interfere with the trial and retained the classicist's view that offenders were rational entities. The neo-classicists introduced the notion of 'mitigating circumstances', thereby permitting background and psychological differences to be considered before sentences were passed. The neo-classicists grafted on to classical theory their own special view of man. Man was still held to be accountable for his actions, albeit with certain minor reservations, but was no longer the isolated, atomistic rational man of pure classicism.

Once classicism began to be diluted, it became a short step to question the offender's rationality at the time the offence was committed. The McNaughton rules were the logical outcome of this type of questioning, allowing a verdict of not guilty by reason of insanity to be passed if the offender was labouring under such a defect of reason as not to know the nature and quality of his acts, or if he did know he did not know that what he was doing was wrong. The emphasis was still on man's reason, and the lack of knowledge of his act constituted the major defence of insanity, and as such, still retained many of the main components of classical theory. Changes in classical theory led to a way of regarding the legal world as something like the following.

> 1. At the centre are adult, sane individuals — seen to be fully responsible for their actions. They are identical to the ideal type actors of 'pure' classical theory — except that some cognizance is taken of their particular circumstances. These allowances are relevant only to mitigation — they do not form the basis of excusing the actor his responsibility . . . .
> 2. Children and (often) the aged are seen to be less capable of making accountable decisions.
> 3. A small group of individuals — the insane and grossly feeble minded — are seen to be incapable of adult freedom of action [With these groups] actions are determined: there is no question of the actors being responsible for what they do . . . .[2]

The outcome was to create a role for people who could inform the court about the offender's past and future, and decide if he was rational enough to be held accountable for the current offence. The psychosocial expert had been launched.

The launching was at first modest, but soon became a more sophisticated exercise. Descriptive accounts of the offender's background quickly gave way to asking questions about the relevance of these backgrounds. Perhaps some features were more relevant than others? If so, which, and in what way? How could an expert decide if an offender was guilty but insane? Clearly more knowledge was needed than could be provided by current jurisprudence. Neo-classicism may have provided the entree but it did not provide the knowledge base with which the experts would later operate. That base came from an altogether different source — a source based on the nineteenth century view of the world dominated by the demands of science. The base was positivism, which incidentally helped to produce the new study of criminology.

Positivism claimed to apply scientific methods to the study of criminals and to the effects of the penal sanctions. Positivists were not concerned with crime; their introduction to the courts was through the criminals, who provided the initial material for their study.

Positivists became accepted because they claimed to be scientific, and few legal jurists could resist a scientific approach when science had so obviously produced such riches in other areas of life. Science, however, is by its nature an infinite exercise and the positivists were rarely content to permit their discipline to be restricted by a legal philosophy based on non-scientific assertions. The relationship between the positivists and neo-classicists has never been harmonious and as positivism developed it soon attacked the foundations of neo-classicism which had helped to produce it. The neo-classicists retained their original view, still defining crime in legal terms, still focusing on crime as a legal entity and still emphasizing rationality as the basis for prosecution. The positivists on the other hand began to reject the legal definition of crime, and focused on crime as a socio-psychological entity. They also emphasized determinism.[3] The tension inherent in these differences is still present today, with the positivists steadily campaigning for a scientific deterministic approach to crime and the neo-classicists valiantly preserving what the positivists call the metaphysics of free will and 'mens rea'.

Positivism had a certain appeal. It also had certain strengths. The first and most obvious strength was that it stressed the value of observation of the facts instead of mere speculation. In so doing it reduced the metaphysical content of criminology and reduced the armchair philosopher to a subordinate role. The facts were important, said the positivists, and the facts should be allowed to speak for themselves. A side effect of this emphasis on facts has been the development of statistics and research methodologies which made these subjects a necessary adjunct to criminology. The facts had to be collected and analysed, so the inferential statistician became indispensable. Criminology then became an empirical science, producing research studies and information. Stan Cohen may see these as having a 'depressing sameness' but he is also right to applaud the ingenuity that produced them.[4] The difficulty is that positivists rarely questioned the nature of these facts; they were simply there, resembling what Durkheim called in a different context the 'things' to be collected in the social world.

Positivism's second strength was that it concentrated on the offender. In other words, it individualized criminals. This produced an apparent sense of equality of consideration as each offender was seen to be different, each having his individual reasons for committing crime. Individualization then became a key element in positivist thinking. This did not stop positivists from developing 'Laws' about human behaviour based on individual observations since the requirements of science insist on such laws. Neither did it mean that the offender became a real person. What the offender had to say was interpreted as something else, the true meaning was imposed on his actions by the scientist. Furthermore, the offender's function was limited, often reduced to giving monosyllabic answers to a pre-coded structured schedule. In classical criminology the offender never said anything either. Although not a statistic or a percentage, he was seen by the classicists as a calculating machine able to decide rationally on courses of action. Furthermore, his apparent rationality avoided legal considerations of the social inequalities surrounding him. As Taylor, Walton and Young say 'Utilitarianism, therefore, was not a theory of unqualified or unrestricted individual equality. Although men were seen to be equal in the sense of having an equal power to reason, they could not be seen (in a propertied society) to be equal in all other respects.'[5]

The third strength of positivism was that it gave the impression that something could be done to prevent crime. The lack of theoretical content in Sheldon and Eleanor Glueck's 'multiple factor theory' has been by-passed for decades because it gave the impression that once factors were identified they could be manipulated in some way. Prevention may have been illusory but that never stopped the Gluecks demonstrating that certain factors were 'causes', and that these factors could be demonstrated as 'causes' by the use of statistical techniques. Tease out the factors, find out which are causal, manipulate these, and hey presto, no more crime. In practice the method has not been all that effective but as long as a scientific posture is maintained impressions are given that something is happening, and that something will eventually reduce crime.

All experts are positivists, all are involved in psycho-social manipulations. Having adopted a positivist stance they require an ever widening knowledge base which will provide more information about the factors requiring manipulation. Once factors are identified, manipulation can take place 'clinically', i.e. by assessment backed up by psycho-social tests such as IQ tests, etc. Surrounding the expert are groups of mini-experts feeding information to him, all accepting the positivist theories, but relying inevitably on the clinician's ability to make the ultimate diagnosis and suggest the ultimate treatment plan.

Although positivism has been described as providing the knowledge base for the experts, this is only partially true. In practice, positivism could more accurately be described as a stance, or a theoretical posture. The real knowledge base of the experts came from psycho-analysis which in this context is a generic term covering a whole host of theories based on unconscious mechanisms. The growth of psycho-analysis was timely but it led to a peculiarly medical twist to the way in which positivism developed in criminology. The psycho-analytic position was obviously tailor-made; it had the displaced status accorded to the medical world and it produced the obvious theoretical basis for methods of diagnosis and treatment. Sociology had value too, but this was not discovered until much later and by then sociological factors could only be seen as secondary and could only be included as an adjunct to the main theme of individual motivation.

Psycho-analysis was timely for other reasons too. First it emphasized, or at least articulated, a growing demand to understand the inner man, a position which led Bertrand Russell to complain of the growing influences of the subjective element in nineteenth century ethics. Freud was very much a product of his time, reflecting in a very powerful way the disillusionment with purely 'external' theories of behaviour. Freud claimed to be a scientist and so was able to reflect concern for the inner man but still retain the groundswell of the scientific posture.[6]

Second, although primarily a medical model using medical terminology, psycho-analysis did not have to be confined to medically qualified practitioners. Lay analysts were soon in practice, guided of course by their medical mentors. In other words, with a little training others could do it provided that they shared the basic assumptions and had the right sort of personality, although some people of course could do it better than others.

Social workers could certainly do it. Scott Briar and Henry Miller trace the origins of the relationship between psycho-analysis and social work to America in the First World War.[7] The war brought with it the mysterious 'disease' called shell shock, and the work of Freud offered an explanation for this puzzling phenomenon. At the same time the Mental Hygiene Movement had begun to attract attention and at the National Conference of Social Workers in 1919, Mary Jarratt read a paper entitled 'The Psychiatric thread running through all casework'. She claimed that 50 per cent of the social workers' cases had a psychiatric orientation. 'Think of what this will do for us', said Miss Jarratt; 'clients on social agencies have mental disorders of various kinds, the psychiatric point of view will give casework an inroad into the vast mental hygiene movement, it will give casework a new objectivity; moreover it will give the poor overworked caseworker an easier job.'

Jessie Taft describes the 1919 Conference held at Atlanta City in more graphic terms:

[The conference] was a landslide for mental hygiene . . . . In every section psychiatrists appeared on the programme. The psychiatric social worker was present in person for the first time and violent indeed was the discussion which raged about her devoted head. What should be her training, what her personality, and what the limitations of her province? Should she remain forever different from other caseworkers, or should every other caseworker be reborn in her likeness?

That was the meeting which burst its bonds and had to be transferred to a church a block away. Dignified psychiatrists and social workers climbed out of windows in order to make sure of a good seat.[8]

A similar change took place in Britain too, although with much less fervour and for slightly different reasons.[9] In a few years Jessie Taft's question was answered, as practically the whole profession had succeeded 'in changing the garments of charity for a uniform borrowed from the practitioners of psycho-analysis'.[10] The link was complete and psycho-analysis had a new army of supporters able to carry the message to a wider social arena. Probation officers in Britain found no difficulty in acquiring that particular psycho-analytic garment. Within a comparatively short space of time the concept of rehabilitation — linked of course to psycho-analytic theories — became the centrepiece of the experts' position. Whereas crime had once been a question for the offender's conscience, or even about morality, it suddenly became a psycho-social phenomena. 'Whilst the doctor treats the body, the soul doctor treats the not-body' is how Professor Flew sums up the position.[11]

Of course, psycho-analysis was not the only knowledge base. It may have been the centrepiece but other theories were, and still are, considered. They too fit neatly into the positivist mould. Whereas psycho-analysts see crime as a product of early familial relationships, others see it as inborn and others as a product of peer group relationships. All, however, share the same common thread: explanations are sought in terms of the criminals, and criminals are in Matza's 'constrained', i.e. all positivist theories postulate differences between offenders and non-offenders, so that each group may be constrained but by different circumstances. Non-offenders are constrained by non-criminal definition, offenders by criminal definitions. The difficulty, says Matza, is that having posited differences between the two groups, no one has ever been able to demonstrate what these differences are.

Experts are structurally located at the 'professional' levels of society. To see them as a homogeneous group is perhaps misleading, for there are many sub-categories. For our purposes, two groups can be delineated; one, the psychiatrist claiming additional medical knowledge and the other the probation officer concerned with social work but sharing many of the psychiatrist's values. The psychiatrist is the more interesting of the two because his role has developed to the point where he is the true expert, able to claim the status of an expert witness in court, able to write confidential reports which contain medical information, and able also to make legitimated pronouncements about 'mental illness'. Probation officers, though more numerous, have a less embracing and exalted position.

A relatively small number of psychiatrists work in the penal system and most of those work on a part-time basis. No one knows how many are involved or what proportion of their time is spent treating offenders. Many prison medical officers have no psychiatric training, although for our purposes it is convenient to classify these as psychiatrists as they tend to operate in that capacity. Given the small number of psychiatrists actually involved on a full-time basis with the treatment of offenders, it is all the more interesting that their influence should be so widespread.

Psychiatrists operating within the penal system seem to have three major roles.[12] First, within the framework of the criminal law they are called to give evidence to the court on the mental state of the accused person, and in particular to the degree to which the accused can be held responsible and therefore punishable for their actions. (This role should not be confused with the pre-sentence medical report to be discussed in chapter 5.) Psychiatric evidence on the state of the accused is most likely to be required in severe cases such as murder, where the punishment is fixed by law, although not exclusively so. The nature of this evidence need not concern us here; the important point surrounds the implication of the psychiatric role, which is described by Barbara Wootton as tainting the medical with the penal. Wootton suggests that psychiatrists are expected to decide whether the accused is healthy enough to be punished, and given the present state of knowledge of mental health she suggests that he is unable to do so without recourse to his own values and ethical position. She also believes that psychiatrists are expected to make valid decisions about other people's responsibility, and she rightly asks if this is ever possible. Can anyone ever say that a person could have acted otherwise than as he did? This is no new problem; it was posed in the nineteenth century by Fitzjames Stephen when he doubted if anyone could decide if an 'irresistible impulse' meant 'an impulse that was not resisted'. The same point was made by Lord Chief Justice Parker in the 1960s when he said the difference between 'he did not resist his impulse' and 'he could not resist his impulse' is one incapable of scientific proof. [13]

Disputes between psychiatrists in courts over the question of the mental state of the accused person and the degree to which he is held responsible is never an edifying experience, particularly for the offender. Abraham Blumberg is direct and says that 'psychiatric evidence is up for sale'.[14] That resolute critic Dr Szasz regards the procedure as damaging to the profession as a whole, although of course he is specifically concerned with the American system.

It is unlikely that toxicologists would be tolerated in Courts of Law if one would assert that he found a large quantity of arsenic in the body fluids of a diseased person and another would state that he found by the allegedly same operation, none. Yet the sorry spectacle is commonplace as regards to psychiatric findings.[15]

A sorry spectacle indeed, but one that happens all too frequently, and in Britain too.[16]

The second way in which the psychiatrist can influence the penal system is at the pre-sentence stage, where psychiatrists recommend that some offenders are more suitable for medical treatment than penal treatment.[17] Briefly there are a number of legal routes which can lead to an offender being treated medically. The most important, as far as the number of offenders is concerned, is Section 60 of the Mental Health Act, which allows a court to make a hospital order on the evidence of two doctors that the offender is suffering from mental illness, subnormality, severe-subnormality or psychopathic disorder which warrants his detention in a hospital for medical treatment. About 1,370 persons were made subject to hospital orders in 1970, which accounted for just over 47 per cent of all 'official methods' of disposing of disordered offenders.

The next most important route — numerically speaking — is by way of Section 4 of the 1948 Criminal Justice Act, which provides for special requirements to be inserted in a probation order requiring the offender for a period of not more than 12 months to submit to psychiatric treatment. The treatment may be either in a mental hospital or as an out-patient. These Section 4 orders account for a further 38 per cent of the official methods. About half of these orders contain in-patient requirements. Taken together, the hospital orders and Section 4 probation orders account for about 85 per cent of all official methods. The remaining 15 per cent is made up of transfers from prison to mental hospitals (e.g. under Section 72, which accounts for a further 7 per cent) and as a result of being found insane on arraignment; not guilty by reason of insanity; infanticide; and on grounds of diminished responsibility (8 per cent).[18]

The psychiatrist's role raises two important questions. The first concerns the nature of his evidence, and the second his position 'vis-à-vis' the offender patient. The first question is part of a wider on-going debate which though important and relevant is more a subject for medical than sociological enquiry. The second question is more appropriate for us here. It is simply this, has the role of the psychiatrist as a decision maker for the courts become a radical departure from his usual medical doctor/patient role? The reply must be an unequivocal yes. Whereas traditionally the function of the doctor has been to attend to the medical needs of his patient, now we suddenly find a branch of the medical profession acting as an agent for the state and making decisions about the patient which do not necessarily have the patient's approval.

It could be argued that such a change is only part of a wider series of changes in the doctor/patient relationships which pervade the whole of the medical profession. To some extent this is true. GPs are acting as agents for the state when they issue medical certificates for sickness benefits, and they act for insurance companies when they give examinations to prospective candidates. Are not psychiatrists operating on similar lines? To some extent yes; the difference is not one of degree but of theoretical posture. An applicant for a life insurance is well aware that the doctor is acting for the insurance company but a person being treated or being subject to a recommendation for hospital treatment is never sure whose side the psychiatrist is on.[19] Few offenders would consider a hospital order or even recognize that they need that type of help. More likely, they would prefer the most lenient sentence which could be, say, a fine. Help, and concern for the offender, in this instance becomes a cloak for acting as an agent of social control. To the question 'whose side are these psychiatrists on?' the answer is simple: on the side of the state which employs them, and no one, least of all the offender, should think otherwise. Psychiatrists who believe themselves competent enough to decide whether a person is fit to stand trial are not necessarily acting according to the wishes of the offender. More likely they are acting according to the requirements of a wider socio-legal arena. Where they do so, at least their role should be spelt out clearly, or as Barbara Wootton says 'if the profession is to assume what are essentially corrective rather than therapeutic functions it is surely important that they should be done openly and not by any specious pretence . . . .'[20] Regrettably, the language of the rehabilitative ideal encourages a 'specious pretence' particularly if there is no recognition of a clash of interests between offender and state, or if no conflict is ever recognized in the notion of being 'sentenced to receive help'.

The point can be put another way, for it has important implications for this aspect of rehabilitation and about how it operates within the penal system. In a crude sense, social control can operate either overtly, i.e. in full view of all parties concerned, or covertly as with the 'specious pretence' described by Barbara Wootton. In practice psychiatrists operate under both systems but tend if anything to be more covert. As social control agents they influence policy by claiming to be experts (the claim is of course accepted), they recommend detention in a mental hospital, and in some instances are asked for their opinion as to the fitness of the defendant to stand trial. The conflict comes when the defendant sees, and is encouraged to see, the psychiatrist as his own medical representative when the reality is different. The social control element occurs when the psychiatrist acts for the state and against the wishes of his patient as can happen when detention in a hospital is recommended or a defendant is refused the right to stand trial as a result of his mental condition. To argue that the decision is ultimately made in the best interests of the defendant is specious, for rights which are opposed or removed are expressions of social control irrespective of these justifications. It is a basic right in British justice to be tried for an alleged offence, and to have that right removed is a serious matter. Psychiatric evidence is of paramount importance in these proceedings, thereby placing the psychiatrist in a position of considerable power. It is surely misplaced to see this influence and power as anything other than social control, but such a change in the doctor/patient relationship ought not to go unnoticed, and as Barbara Wootton says, 'such a change would perhaps have shocked Hippocrates'.[21]

The third way the psychiatrist can influence the penal system is less formal but no less pervasive. It relates to their earlier role as the teachers of probation officers and others operating a therapeutic relationship. The effect has been to produce a sense of awe about what psychiatrists could or could not do, although in recent years psychiatrists have lost some of this reverence. It is not clear why this recent change has taken place, although the earlier position has by no means completely vanished and there are still few courses for trainee probationers without a psychiatrist in attendance.[22]

The implications of this 'training' role are widespread.[23] Under this psychiatric influence court officials have been encouraged to see penal measures in some form of conceptual hierarchy. This means that non-reformist measures are to be avoided (i.e. fines, suspended sentence, etc.) whilst measures involving therapy should be promoted. Since legal definitions like all other definitions are subject to influence, this indicates that they are potential targets for change.[24] Rehabilitationists know this and constantly attempt to redefine penal issues in their language. Probation officers do so too, so that even a prison can become ' a structured environment', and probation is certainly regarded as 'a means of support'.The aims are not to deceive the offender who may have access to this language, nor are they written to soften the blow of the reality of the sentence, although one cannot of course discount these aspects. More likely they are attempts to redefine institutions in therapeutic terms so that once redefined the institution itself will appear to *approximate* to those definitions. Redefinitions also give entrees and higher status to the defining group.

The difficulty of course is that the key word is 'approximate'. Institutions tend to have a life of their own and once they become operative and move in a certain direction it is difficult to alter that course. Social structures become ossified and organizational demands become paramount. By changing a name one may change the functioning.

But by changing a name one may falsely imply that a particular function has been changed. So padded cells may remain in mental hospitals but they become 'rooms for solitary contemplation', cold showers on a winter's morning become 'hydro-therapy' and work becomes 'occupational therapy'. These linguistic changes may not of themselves be important were it not for the fact that they hide the reality. Francis Allen puts the point well when he says that,

> under the dominance of the rehabilitative ideal the language of therapy is frequently employed, wittingly or unwittingly to disguise the true state of affairs that prevails in our custodial institutions and at other points in the correctional process.[25]

Weschsler makes a similar observation when he says that there are many coercive regimes we would not accept if they were openly called punitive but are tolerated if called therapeutic even though no therapy is done there.[26] With this in mind we should not ignore Francis Allen's warning that there is a strong tendency for the rehabilitative ideal to serve purposes that are essentially incapacitative rather than therapeutic in character.

The psychiatrist's influence on the probation service has provided a powerful effect in promoting rehabilitative measures and ideologies. Probation officers may not have the overt power of the psychiatrists, being unable to commit people to mental hospitals or even act as expert witnesses in the courts, but they have been able to influence attitudes, particularly among the judiciary ('educate the magistrates' is an oft used phrase). They have a symbiotic relationship with the judiciary which gives them influence if not power and it is this influence which sets them apart from other social workers. They can advise the courts on sentencing practice, apply to courts for warrants for breaches of probation, and advise the after-care authorities, including the parole board, about an ex-offender's behaviour on after-care or parole. Their advice will be taken seriously and ex-offenders can be recalled if an adverse report is sent about them. They constantly act out the language of the therapists but differ from the psychiatrist as being members of a large bureaucracy. Psychiatrists are more likely to be self-employed or at least have a more professional identity.

Treatment in the community as far as adult offenders are concerned means that the probation service will be involved at some stage or another. For juveniles under the age of 17, community treatment is more widespread and involves local authority social workers who have children on supervision orders, are responsible for care orders and for intermediate treatment. With adults, the probation service reigns supreme, with the trend toward increasing its influence rather than decreasing it. The 1972 Criminal Justice Act extended the range of sentences to include community service orders, day training centres, bail and other hostel provisions, and postponements of sentences, all of which tend to increase the probation service's influence.[27]

The Morrison Committee defined probation as 'the submission of an offender while at liberty to a specified period of supervision by a social caseworker who is an officer of the court; during the period the offender remains liable, if not of good conduct, to be otherwise dealt with by the Court'. This definition of course tells us little about the objectives, and hides many of the subtleties that exist in probation. It also gives the impression of a predominantly legal approach divorced from the usual realms of psycho-analytic theory although of course it does mention the 'social caseworker'. Jarvis gives a far more comprehensive account.

> The professional practice of probation is directed towards the achievement of more permanent goals than inhibition under authoritative restraint of criminal or otherwise anti-social conduct during the limited period of recognizance. The techniques of intensive casework counselling and recourse to general community resources are exploited to their fullest extent in an endeavour to develop within the probationer those qualities of character and personality which lead to the permanent assumption of a stable and responsible manner of living.[28]

Probation then is not just aimed at reducing criminality but to do 'something more', and that something more is, according to Jarvis, character formation, aimed at providing 'a stable and responsible manner of living'. Irrespective of the possibility of achieving these goals, there is in the definition a whole series of moral judgments, not the least that stability and responsibility are to be seen as ends in themselves. Szasz in a similar vein makes the point that when a psychiatrist who advises a married couple contemplating divorce that they should have a child, or cultivate a common interest, he is not an agent of either man or wife but rather an agent of marriage as a social institution.[29] The probation officer likewise when requiring stability and responsibility for his client is acting as an agent of the status quo, or more particularly one section of that status quo, which in this sense means the courts.

Obviously Jarvis' definition will not be acceptable to all probation officers; some would undoubtedly object to terms like 'stability' and probably be more concerned with 'adjustment'. Few, however, would object to the notion of 'intensive counselling' as one of the major means, a goal which is well established in almost all probation officers' minds before they complete their training.

In one of the few major studies of probation officers' attitudes towards this work, almost all gave casework goals as their major theoretical orientation. Eighty-four probation officers were asked whether they attached high or low importance to various factors in the treatment of probation.[30] The results are given in Tables 3.1 and 3.2.

Table 3.1

Assessment of probationers and the environment	No. of officers rating the factor as:	
	High	Low
The offender's personality	81	3
Degree of emotional adjustment	78	6
Family	84	0
Clubs	8	76

The emphasis here is on rather classical casework principles with personality and emotional adjustment within the family scoring high ratings. There was a similar agreement about the aims of probation.

Table 3.2

	High	Low
Punishment	3	81
Rehabilitation	83	1
Participation in clubs	8	76
Emotional adjustment	82	2

Rehabilitation and emotional adjustment were rated highly and illustrate a general consensus about the overall aims. There were disagreements about the way in which these aims could be realized although clarification by discussion and discussion of family problems showed a similarly high rating. Disagreements existed about the values of intelligence, work, etc., as a means to achieving these goals. This table emphasizes that the major focus of probation involves clinical evaluation of personality which is theoretically grounded on traditional social work principles.

But in fact probation differs from traditional social work in a number of other respects; first, in its link with the courts and its authoritarian setting, and second, by the duties imposed on the probation officer by the conditions of the probation order and by powerful organizations such as the Home Office and by local probation committees. These differences have not gone unnoticed but the dilemma is usually solved by superimposing the authoritarian duty on the case-work ethic. In an article by S.R. Eshelby, a principal probation officer, the dilemma appears to be neatly solved:

> Today's probation officer would have no difficulty in defining his work to fit most delineations of casework, for example [Bowers] 'social casework is an act in which knowledge of the science of human relations and the skill in relationship are used to mobilize capacities in the individual and resources in the community appropriate for better adjustment between the client and all or any part of his total environment.' The probation officer seeks to do this in his supervisory work, though he may attempt to do other things as well, such as discipline his clients, which may put him outside the fold of caseworkers.[31]

Apart from the absurdity of Bowers's definition (which in another context led Barbara Wootton to remark that to live up to these or similar aims the caseworker would have to marry the client), and apart from Eshelby saying that probation officers live up to Bowers's definition *and do other things as well,* there is no apparent recognition of any theoretical conflict. Mark Monger in a more realistic vein notes that the court making a probation order is 'a definite exercise in authority'.[32]

Probation differs from other social work by the presence of legal rules and conditions attached to them. These rules and conditions legitimize the probation officer's authority. No one can be on probation without the presence of these formal rules. There are usually three standard conditions attached to each probation order and the order can be made for a period not exceeding three years.

1. To be of good behaviour and lead an industrious life.
2. To inform the probation officer at once of any change of residence or employment.
3. To keep in touch with the probation officer in accordance with such instructions as may from time to time be given by the probation officer, and in particular, if the probation officer so requires,

to receive visits from the probation officer at home.
Other conditions can be inserted but as the offender has to agree to be
placed on probation additional conditions are also subject to the
offender's agreement. Some pose their own problems of enforcement,
particularly where conditions are attached which, say, order the
offender to 'keep away from thieves and other undesirables' or 'keep
away from strong drink'. Technically, a breach of any of these conditions can lead to an application by the probation officer to return
the offender to court to be sentenced again for the original offence or
dealt with in a way which still allows the probation order to continue.

The very looseness of the language used in the conditions is designed
to permit flexibility, but has the equally obvious effect of permitting
individual interpretation by each probation officer. In a current
research project by the author, concerned with breaches of probation,
early results suggest that all offenders break some conditions of their
order, but the definition of these infractions as a serious deviant act
varies enormously. In other words the chances of being returned to
court depend on the theoretical perspectives of the individual officers,
or to put it another way, it depends on those who invent, modify and
enforce the norms.

Probation officers and the Probation Service have of course benefited
from this special relationship with the courts. Their own status is a
reflected one and reflected by fiat. But of course fiat status presents its
own problems, not the least being that once acquired there is a reluctance to lose it. In practice this means that role conflicts and ideological
conflicts have to be reduced to a minimum. Whenever fiat status exists
we can expect that the eventual aim is harmonization or an attempt to
achieve participation through partnership. Conflict can be reduced by
superficially adopting the values of the high status group. At a deeper
level, conflict may remain but probation officers tend to reduce this
by a process of gentle persuasion demonstrated in their constant
reference to 'educating the magistrates'. The overall effect of fiat
status, however, is more invidious and it is now recognized by many
critics that the partnership with the courts has meant the dilution of
probation idealism. What was once a radical alternative to an apparently
insensitive penal system has sadly become an institutionalized feature
of the very organization it attempted to change. It may have influenced
the court as regards the therapeutic ideology but has lost the opportunity to do more than this — or at least become more radical and affect
the basic structure.

The outcome was of course fairly predictable; the courts, which
admit no superior authority except Parliament, were unlikely to change
radically. Any outside group, posing an alternative ideology, yet
dependent on the courts for its clients, would inevitably have to

compromise and those compromises would also inevitably have to be in the court's favour. In America the position is even worse for while probation officers are still 'officers of the court', Blumberg sees them as 'hand maidens' lacking the service ideal which professional status implies because they are too firmly allied to the organization of the court:

> Probation journals and probation workers' organizations emphasize the professional nature of probation work. Like the funeral director, the hospital administrator, the accountant and the social worker, the probation officer has attempted to professionalize. But he has tried to do so by fiat rather than by developing a special body of technical knowledge. The self image of the probation officer as a professional is seriously negated by his lack of autonomy in the court organization.[33]

Blumberg may be overstating the case for Britain but status by fiat has produced a lack of independent development. It is also beginning to produce a loss of credibility in the eyes of the clients who are now seeing probation officers in the same terms as they see other court officials, i.e. as people to be used when the occasion arises but who remain fundamentally different from them. Criticism of probation officers by clients is more widespread now than ever before and such a change should not go unnoticed.

With its hierarchy of statuses, probation is a career, offering its own career progression. It is also organized as a public bureaucracy containing within it the special elements of bureaucratic control. To some extent the whole nature of a bureaucracy is antithetical to the rehabilitative ideal which probation officers are expected to practice. We need go no further than Max Weber's account of bureaucracies to see this point. Weber saw bureaucratic administration as involving the exercise of control on the basis of the knowledge of the official. This he said produced three general social consequences.

1. The tendency to 'levelling' in the interest of the broadest possible basis of recruitment in terms of technical competence.
2. The tendency to plutocracy growing out of the interest in the greatest possible length of technical training.
3. The dominance of a spirit of formalistic impersonality — without hatred or passion, and hence without affection or enthusiasm. The dominant norms are concepts of straightforward duty without regard to personal considerations. Everyone is subject to formal equality of treatment; that is everyone in the same empirical situation. This is the spirit in which the ideal official conducts his office.[34]

Weber's analysis is relevant for a number of different reasons. Although he was concerned with the officials themselves, Weber thought that official norms affected the methods of processing the clients. In short, bureaucracies require technical competence; they reward training; they produce a formalistic impersonality and they produce formal equality of treatment. Rehabilitation on the other hand, requires *individual* attention and flexibility, neither of which is suitable for bureaucratic organizations. Rehabilitation also requires 'flair' but bureaucracies require formalistic impersonality 'without affection or enthusiasm'. Bureaucracies also have a tendency to develop plutocracies so that the most competent get promoted. So, it is the least competent, i.e. the basic grade probation officers, who are left to make contact with the clients.

The thrust towards plutocracies is a well known bureaucratic phenomenon, but the argument has a peculiar twist as far as the personal social services are concerned. What is the effect on newly appointed probation officers of entering this bureaucracy, particularly as probation recruits are usually idealistic people with a sense of vocation and concern about welfare and about people's problems? Surely this poses a dilemma? On the one hand recruitment programmes encourage the idealism. 'Do you care enough about people?' is the standard opening line of the probation service's recruiting campaign. Initial training courses support the idealism emphasizing the 'caring' and the 'changing' elements in social work whether the change is a change in the clients personality or in society. The trained probation officer on appointment will often consider himself a specialist in the whole range of 'people work' capable of changing people, or changing society or both. The presumption is fostered by the idealistic nature of the theories of social work and of the literature which constantly discusses 'growth' and 'change'. On appointment the reality shock is powerful and idealism soon becomes translated into career advancement and promotion. Geoffrey Parkinson notes how the new recruit quickly prepares to catch the principal's eye and waits to move up the hierarchy. In doing so he may change his idealism for a bureaucratic approach but what happens to that original idealism? Promotion will of course be ideologically justified on the grounds that the real decisions are made at a higher level. This is of course manifestly true but career advancement was presumably not the reason for joining, and at least not part of the recruitment programme. Inherent in all bureaucracies is a strong component of social control which stands in marked contrast to the idealism of the trainee with flair and imagination and who sees his work as being involved in social and personality change.

But what of the experts' success, or rather, how is success measured or determined? Criminologists have debated the question of determining success and have reluctantly accepted that no reliable measurement is available. They often rely on further convictions as a form of measurement. Hood and Sparks show that success measured in these terms is a crude and unsophisticated method primarily because further convictions are so heavily dependent on police activity.[35] For example, D.J. West's study of the habitual prisoner shows that 'crime free periods' ought to be more accurately described as 'prosecution free', for crimes were still being committed but no one was caught.[36] Probation officers typically reject further convictions as an index of success. In one sense they are obviously right to do so, but they do not reject them always on these same grounds. Probation officers claim to be doing 'something more' and this 'something more' is related to their ideological approach described in the Home Office Research Project, i.e. as having an effect on the offender's personality and on his emotional adjustment. Presumably psychiatrists also claim to be doing 'something more' but with mental hospital patients they have to be involved in curing the mental illness in addition to the social and psychological goals of the probation officers.

A clear cut idea of what constitutes success obviously should be crucial, for offenders can only be discharged from hospital, prison or from their probation order when they have successfully completed treatment. The aims and methods of rehabilitation are relatively clear but in a curious way there is hardly any discussion of successful completion. Probation orders finish by the court's decree, i.e. a person is on probation for a specified period of time so probation ends when the probation order ends. But how does a probation officer decide if the probationary period has been 'successful'? And how, and by what criteria does a psychiatrist decide when to release a person from hospital?

There is not so much a shortage of literature on the subject as a deafening silence. Lydia Rapaport stands out as one of the few social workers to discuss this issue and then only briefly and tangentially. 'Termination obviously is intrinsically linked with the formulation of specific goals. It takes place when a specifically defined goal has been reached. *That may or may not be easily determined.*' (Italics mine.)[37]

Unfortunately she tells us no more. There is no discussion on specific goals but there is at least some sensitivity to the problem that a definition of goals may not be easily determined. To say that the issue is crucial is not to overstate the case, for decisions about successful treatment were certainly crucial to George Jackson, as they are to people already in mental hospitals, and as they would be to anyone who was to be judged as reformed.

How, then, are decisions made about successful treatments? No one appears to know, but quite clearly they are not made outside the realms of values and moral judgments. Inevitably decisions are based on what Szasz calls the overt values in psychiatric assessment, and what C. Wright Mills sees as the acceptable standards of middle class small town Americans. To be rehabilitated means that an offender is fit to take his place in the world again, but whose world is this? Presumably the world of the independent, career orientated, happily married, tension free professional, not the world of the hobo, drug addict, criminally deviant or activist revolutionary. If a sense of independence is a criteria, we can be sure that this does not mean acquiring more money from Supplementary Benefits; it means not having to resort to Supplementary Benefits at all. Similarly a career does not mean a criminal career but a legitimate one based on all the trappings of promotion, status and consumer values. Perhaps the reformed are a little like the experts themselves . . . .

Now there is nothing inherently wrong with advocating a legitimate career, or wanting people to be happy or even helping them to have a happy marriage. What is wrong is to suggest that people who achieve this have been successfully 'treated'. Happiness is not a neutral quality, it belongs more appropriately to the world of moral philosophy than to the world of medical models. Happiness also implies the existence of an agreed normative framework and if so, then we can be certain that the framework is not wildly different from the expert's own life experiences.

Sociologists like C. Wright Mills can be excused for jumping to conclusions about some of the aims of treatment particularly if the experts themselves rarely discuss the nature of success or do not bother to refute the pungent criticisms of these writers. However, in my own probation study concerned with the early discharge of probation orders for 'good progress' it did not appear possible to specify components of successful treatment but some generalizations could be made about the reverse. An offender was not likely to get an early discharge if he had been convicted of another offence, if he had not been in regular work, if he had discordant personal relationships, e.g. a difficult marriage, and if he failed to report regularly. Nor was he likely to get an early discharge if he refused to accept that he had been helped by the probation officer. Offenders had to accept emphatic insights (i.e. if there is a disagreement it means the offender needed more treatment) in order to demonstrate the value of probation. No wonder offenders learn that experts need to be told what they want to hear.

It is more difficult to assess the work of psychiatrists because their records are less flamboyant. Details of discharge procedures are rarely recorded and it is possible for a patient to be discharged without any reference to his mental condition. It appears that decisions to discharge a patient involve two factors: the psychiatric and the social. The second may influence the first: so for example, a person with a home to go to could well be released earlier than someone without settled accommodation, but it is not always clear how and under what circumstances this operates.

The really frightening feature of this whole area is that no one appears to have been concerned about spelling out the necessary conditions which a patient would have to fulfil before being released. When questioned on these issues psychiatrists typically reply that release is possible when the patient is symptom free. Unfortunately, this is another deceptively simple answer. At the extremes, as in schizophrenia, the answer has some relevance, as a patient could be released when he no longer hallucinates. Experts, however, typically deal with less florid behaviour patterns than exist with schizophrenics, their routine criminal cases show few signs of 'mental illness' in the usual definitional sense of that term. The most that can be said of the bulk of their patients is that they are 'disturbed'. How does a psychiatrist know when someone is no longer 'disturbed' or even when he is less disturbed than before, or perhaps still too disturbed to be let out at all?

There are no answers to these questions, and presumably it is no accident that few experts are prepared to discuss the matter. At the risk of being repetitive, it is important to note that the literature overflows with discussions on diagnosis, assessment, and treatment plans, all of which deal with admissions to the hospitals but no one appears to discuss questions about release. Who gets let out, when and for what reasons, are no less important than who gets admitted, when and for what reasons. Both sets of questions deeply affect personal liberty and are too important to be left to experts who see the questions as based on technical competence.

Consider one particular example. Assume that a person is in a mental hospital having been convicted of murder. Assume also an indeterminate sentence with powers given to the psychiatrist to decide when to release the patient. The decision will imply that the psychiatrist will be certain that the man will not kill again. Now, can anyone ever be certain that no one will ever kill again? Statistically, few people are convicted of murder more than once, but there is no technique yet devised which will provide an accurate prediction, and presumably no such technique will *ever* be devised. Francis Allen describes a similar case of a man in his eighties who had been thirty years in a penal institution having killed his wife whilst drunk but having been committed after being found insane. An elderly sister of the offender was able and willing to provide him with a home and the man was eager to leave the institution.

Allen continues:

> When we asked the director of the institution why the old man was
> not released, he gave two significant answers. In the first place the
> statute requires me to find that this inmate is no longer a danger to
> the community; this I cannot do for he may kill again. And, of
> course, the director was right . . . he could not be certain. But as far
> as that goes he could not be certain about you or me. The second
> answer was equally interesting. The old man he said is better off
> here.[38]

Allen is right. The director could not be certain, because no amount
of expertise can provide that sort of predictive capacity. Even if a
prediction table could be devised which gave a predictive score for
the man as having a 99 per cent success rate the director's dilemma is
still not solved. The 1 per cent uncertainty still remains. Perhaps, then,
it is morally indefensible to place such a burden on directors of these
institutions? But it is equally morally indefensible for directors to have
accepted that responsibility in the first place, for the experts have consistently argued that they are the right group to deal with these
patients. In Allen's example this director's second answer was equally
illuminating for he did not appear to have the slightest qualms about
the moral position in which he found himself. To say the old man was
'better off here' is as Allen says a reflection on the 'arrogance and
insensitivity to human values to which men who have no reason to
doubt their own motives appear peculiarly susceptible'.[39]

In the absence of any detailed criteria for deciding on the ends of
treatment we are inevitably forced back to agree with Matza when he
says that decisions involving rehabilitation are based on 'a reliance of
professional judgment'. If this is so, then it is of no surprise to see that
professional judgments produce variations from expert to expert. The
extent of these variations has typically been seen as imposing a
limitation on anyone wanting to study the subject matter, because
reformists suggest that the variations preclude the possibility of making
meaningful generalizations. Matza's reply is that the extent of these
variations are one of the most revealing generalizations one can possibly
make. He is primarily concerned with the way in which dispositions are
recorded in American juvenile courts, but the same argument applies
to decisions about the ends of treatment for adult offenders.

> The inclusion of personal and social character as relevant criteria in
> judgment has been consequential. Its consequence has been that
> hardly anyone, and least of all the recipients of judgment who have
> some special interest in these matters, is at all sure what combination

of the widely inclusive relevant criteria yield what sorts of specific disposition.[40]

How, then, do dispositions get recorded? Matza goes on to say,

> A combination of impoverished economic position, a marginal scholastic record, and particular kind of disrupted family situation, a current infraction of burglary, and two past citations for auto theft yields a disposition. What disposition? If we ask court agents they will honestly and appropriately answer that it all depends. On what does it depend? It depends on other factors. On what other factors? Well, perhaps on a diagnosis of . . . personality, but that too depends. On what does that depend? Ultimately it depends on the needs of the child. And on what do these needs depend? And eventually we come to the final and only possible answer. It depends on the professional training, experience and judgment of the court agents.[41]

Matza's point is that any system with a frame of relevance as wide as that which includes social and personality characteristics of the offender and in which items within that frame of relevance are neither specifically enumerated nor weighted must come to rely heavily on professional judgment. These professional judgments produce what he calls 'rampant discretions' and rehabilitation in Matza's terms involves little else except professional judgments.

This is not the complete picture. Organizational demands can be used to justify changes and variations when the organization is given a degree of flexibility. Borstals operate with relatively indeterminate sentence and as such are overt supporters of rehabilitation. They can release an offender within a period of between six months and two years, and the decision to release him is based on his progress, or put another way on his level of rehabilitation. Unhappily the period of release is also affected by the pressure on places. When there are more borstal sentences the inmate is released quicker. This may be fortunate for those particular inmates but less fortunate if there is not the same pressure to get them discharged quickly. Rehabilitative institutions then become an easy target for the vagaries of policy makers, simply because their ready made flexibility provides policy makers with a convenient target for rapid change. This change may not of course always be in the interests of the offenders, but it certainly solves the problem of having to provide alternative institutions. In this sense rehabilitation could become a convenient tool for the use of state power.

4

TREATMENT ANd THE EXPERTS

In chapter 3, basic questions were asked about the experts. In this chapter, some considerations will be given to the nature of the experts' treatment. What is it and what does it involve? Above all, how successful is it, for in one sense decisions about its value will have to be made on issues which include success.

The world of medicine, and medical practice consists of methods of treatments which usually appear purposeful, and involve 'doing things' to a patient. The patient may not understand the mechanisms involved or even the implications of these methods such as taking temperatures, making charts and prescribing medicines, but he is likely to view the whole process as being more or less in his best interest. He may also note that the world of physical medicine routinely and systematically uses knowledge to make the sufferer better. It is often a suprise to realize that the treatment offered by the rehabilitative experts appears to be substantially different. To the new patient it rarely seems to be based on anything routine or systematic but proceeds at a leisurely pace, only occasionally using physical medical practices such as drugs, or ECT.

In fact rehabilitative treatment consists mainly of talk. To the expert, lengthy discussions about a person's background are regarded as treatment, so are ventilations of anger and accounts of previous social situations. Unhappily, the patient may sometimes see the talk as the preliminaries to the main treatment programme and be surprised to realize that the talk is all the treatment he is ever likely to receive.

Treatment talk is not, however, a haphazard or random conversation, in spite of its appearance to the contrary. It is purposeful, aimed at altering the patient's world view. This world view means in effect a rearrangement of social relationships. The aim is to provide new inter- pretations of the past relationships and/or provide effective management of future ones. The argument behind treatment talk is plausible enough. It is based on the premise that the original world view caused the present offence so a new world view is needed. World views are, however, somewhat expansive and it is no suprise to realize that to the expert everything is relevant. Treatment talk therefore covers every- thing, not just because the expert needs to probe into every facet of the person's life, but in order to discover that particular 'something' which is regarded as the reason behind the current offence and because talk deals with the routines of everyday life. Everything may be relevant but in practical terms 'everything' usually means discussions about parents but not about grandparents, and discussions about siblings but not about cousins, second cousins or aunts. It also means discussion about homes and children but rarely about workmates, football matches, TV, and gardening. Everything may be relevant but some things appear to be more relevant than others.

There is another sense in which treatment talk is not haphazard, and that is that it takes place behind a penal sanction. Rehabilitationists tend to play this down and imply that treatment is voluntarily requested. Penal institutions, however, are autocratic and not institutions which permit the offender a wide range of choices. The person on probation can no more choose his probation officer than the mental patient can choose his psychiatrist, and by the same argument cannot and does not choose his form of treatment. To put the matter crudely, he gets what he is given. Of course a patient gets what he is given in a general hospital too, but the difference is that the patient may have seen the need to go to hospital in the first place. Few people see the need to be placed on probation. It is also curious that whilst the offender may not have asked to be put on probation, and cannot choose his probation officer, none the less he is judged according to whether he has been able to benefit from what he has been given. Ultimately the decision about the form of treatment is taken by the treatment officials, and no one should be misled into thinking otherwise. Experts will sometimes justify their position by arguing that the criminal offence was an unconscious 'cry for help'. Armed with that philosophy it becomes a simple step to see that the expert may not have been formally invited to give his treatment but the offender *really* wanted it anyway. Some experts argue that a 'contract' exists between them and the offender. This is misleading and a misuse of the term contract. There is no free bargaining in the relationship in the sense that free bargaining takes place before a normal contract is made, and no real element of choice. Any 'contract' that might exist is drawn up by the expert, and stated in his terms. The expert dictates the pace, and ultimately decides when the 'contract' has been broken. It cannot be otherwise, for the expert has the power and a statutory duty to enforce controls. 'Treatment' becomes no less an imposition than training; the only difference is that it is usually presented as if training is forcibly imposed whereas treatment is not.

Up to this point the distinction made by Roger Hood between treatment and training has offered a useful working definition (i.e. differences are shown by treatment coming from within the offender, while training is imposed by external controls). It is now convenient to incorporate Herbert Packer's analysis. Packer is concerned specifically with the distinctions between treatment and punishment and so shifts the position slightly.[1] In so doing he gives additional clarity. He begins his analysis by noting that the distinction is often blurred because the concepts are used as if treatment automatically implied that the patient is better off than if he were punished. Packer sees the difference in terms of what he calls two related considerations: (1) the difference in justifying purpose; and (2) the larger role of the offending conduct in the case of punishment. By this he means that the primary purpose of treatment is to benefit the person being treated whereas the justification for punishment is the prevention of undesired conduct. Retribution is justified on the grounds of perceived wrongdoing, justification for treatment is regarded by rehabilitationists as self evident. Confusion in the terminology is compounded when rehabilitationists do not make a distinction between treatment and punishment. To lock up a person or to give him an education in order to prevent him from committing further offences does not, as Packer says, describe the essential difference between treatment and punishment. The essential difference lies in the nature of the relationship between the offending conduct and what we do to the person who has engaged in it.

> Punishment may be more painful than treatment, or it may be less painful; popular opinion to the contrary, *the degree of painfulness does not constitute the difference.* The difference is that in the case of punishment we are dealing with a person because he has engaged in offending conduct, our concern is either to prevent the recurrence of such conduct or to inflict what is thought to be deserved, pain or both. In the case of treatment there is no necessary relation between conduct and treatment; we deal with the person as we do because we think he will be better off as a consequence.[2]

Packer's analysis shows that we should not automatically assume that we are talking about a less painful process if the offender was treated, than if he was punished. Furthermore, hospitalization or even a probation order made on an offender to suit the convenience of others without any representation that the offender will be better off as a consequence is, as Packer says, punishment. The distinction then between the two is found in the aims, even though the methods and the means can be the same.

If we use Packer's arguments then throughout the chapter it will be assumed that whenever treatment is mentioned the aim is always to make the offender better. If treatment fails to achieve these aims then it becomes an empirical question rather than a socio-philosophical one, for a distinction must also be made between the aims and the achievement of these aims.

It is also a convenient point to make one further clarification. The terms 'offender', 'client' and 'patient' have so far been used interchangeably. 'Offender' has been used as a generic term, whilst 'patient' is used when the offender is being treated by a psychiatrist, and 'client' when treated by a social worker. The terms are used in this way by the particular treatment agencies, and it is convenient to continue with this usage.

The first questions, then, are who gives the treatment and what does it involve? In these particular areas rehabilitation has recently come under heavy criticism. The attacks have been directed at two areas First at the point where rehabilitationists operate as if there is an absence of conflict in their relationships between therapist and patient, and second where they say that limits to success are related to trained personnel rather than any inherent theoretical defects. In this chapter I want to use and develop these criticisms and try to show that rehabilitation within the penal system is not based on a harmonious relationship, and furthermore that the question of personnel is a complex one. Where additional personnel have been recruited the success of rehabilitation has still not been demonstrated.

In structural terms, rehabilitation is usually done by middle class professionals on working class offenders. From this basic point, other arguments automatically follow. Inevitably social distance exists at a structural level even before we consider the question of social distance inherent in the treatment model itself. Not all offenders are working class by any means, but middle and upper class offenders are in a minority and probably constitute only about 5 per cent of the experts' caseloads. They also present additional problems described graphically by Goffman when he says that VIPs in a mental hospital have special treatment, even to the point of having their professional titles omitted from the file cards.[3] They have special treatment in probation offices too, rarely having to sit for long periods in waiting rooms with working class criminals, but typically having appointments at unusual hours and having more home visits from the probation officer.[4] These instances, though small in their way, none the less point to a feature of rehabilitation which is usually forgotten; namely, that it operates best when social distance is greatest. Barbara Wootton captured the essence of this point when she asked if casework was so effective, why waste time on the working classes, and why not use it on the world's political leaders? The answer is not difficult to find. The nature of the relationship is based on an ascribed superior-inferior role which the middle classes, and particularly successful members of the middle class, are reluctant to accept.

Social distance stems from the moral overtones inherent in the notion of treatment. The very fact that a person is seen to need rehabilitation implies that he was once habilitated and now needs the process to be repeated. This immediately puts him in a morally inferior position. There is a further assumption of inferiority because without treatment he is regarded as an outsider, and since we, the majority do not apparently require rehabilitation, the offender's status is underlined. This is not all, for the terminology used in treatment and the treatment methods reinforce the sense of inferiority. First consider the terminology.

In all very obvious senses psychiatric diagnoses are moral evaluations, although some are more obviously so than others. The term character disorder exemplifies an extreme moral posture. Presumably those not suffering from – or at least not having – a character disorder, have an ordered character, and there is no moral achievement in having one's character seen as loose or fragmented. Experts would also presumably see their task as straightening it out or tying it up to make it ordered again. A straightened out and tied up character hopefully brings the offender back to the moral position of we normal character ordered people. What does an 'inadequate personality' mean if it is not a moral term? Paul and Patricia de Berker describe the inadequate as a person leading an unfulfilled, poorly organized life which seems to stem from the deficiencies of his personality. The inadequate apparently shows 'an exceptionally low record of competence in work, has an unsatisfactory marital status . . . with frequent marital breakdowns'. De Berker describes these marital breakdowns as resulting from a weak ineffectual man married to a weak woman who is nevertheless more positive in her behaviour'.[5] The overall picture of the inadequate, if de Berker is to be believed, is of a person lacking in drive and purpose. In other words he is inadequate according to those definitions of inadequacy which are themselves in line with values about the merits of drive and purposeful activity. It is difficult not to see these descriptions of personalities as being moral when someone is described as weak and ineffectual.

Moral evaluations not only pervade the diagnostic terminology but typically pervade the treatment plans. Experts may be offering sympathy or even condemnation, but either way they are involved in moral postures which cannot be avoided. Social life essentially consists of judgments about personalities and there is no way of ever avoiding this. That the experts often operate as kind and sensitive to people is all to the good, but this is only because kindness and sensitivity are virtues extolled in our society. Barbara Wootton again captures the essence of this point when she says that psychiatric reports in juvenile courts could have been written by anyone sympathetic toward children, and by this she means that sensitivity is a good thing in itself and that psychiatrists are merely trying to reflect these 'good' values.

Not all observers see the experts as operating with 'good' values. Goffman, for example, may have a jaundiced view but with his usual perceptiveness describes hospital records as being discrediting statements containing scandalous and defamatory remarks. He cites the patient who is described as a man of 'rather neat appearance with a natty Hitlerian moustache'. The patient is also apparently 'a rather gay liver and jim-dandy type of fellow'. He is talkative but 'if he talks long enough on any subject it soon becomes apparent that he is so completely lost in this verbal diarrhoea as to make what he says completely worthless'.[6] It is not necessary then to rely on a diagnosis to label someone as morally inferior; behavioural descriptions work equally well.

Goffman's account is by no means an isolated example. Records of offenders in probation offices and mental hospitals typically use such pejorative descriptions. Functionally these descriptions can be seen as helping to promote social distance by preventing normalization of the deviant act. Matza argues that once deviancy becomes normalized it is difficult to see the offender as requiring rehabilitation. He has a point here, as it is interesting to note that once treatment is successfully completed, normalization occurs and moral assassinations vanish from the records. Offenders are then typically described as relaxed, or healthy, or well groomed and confident, all comparing favourably with earlier descriptions which include a tense, pasty looking individual, or even as in Goffman's example as having a Hitlerian moustache and suffering from verbal diarrhoea.

Although moral overtones are used in all modern methods of treatment talk, they are emphasized and exacerbated when treatment involves offenders. The commission of an offence, with its subsequent additional moral implications, is often enough to underline a person's behaviour as immoral, but when backgrounds are examined and personalities described, the total effect is to produce a constellation of moral disorders each used to support the other. Translated into a treatment programme, rehabilitation in this context means that moral disorder A — which is the offence — is seen as being produced by, or caused by moral disorder B — which is the offender's character and background. In order to treat one moral disorder, say the offence, it becomes necessary to treat the other. Any attempt to escape treatment of the so called character disorder is quickly referred back to the offence disorder. Greater pressure is then placed on the offender to examine his character within the treatment model and within the expert's own terms, for there *must* be something wrong with the character otherwise there would have been no offence in the first place. This is what Goffman means when he says that a large part of psychotherapy consists of holding up the sins of a patient and getting him to see the error of his ways.[7]

Offenders themselves occasionally present the therapist with a legitimate opportunity to be involved in moral evaluations. When they do, they also introduce their own form of social distance and do not force the expert to normalize their behaviour. Legitimate rights to evaluate stem from an acceptance by the offender that it was the offender's personality which caused the offence and that personality needs some form of therapeutic tinkering. Offenders may give accounts of their behaviour in terms of an irresistible impulse such as 'I don't know what came over me.' This is a tacit way of recognizing that they were then behaving abnormally. Alternatively, offenders may cast their past life in terms of a historical build up to the present offence, 'Things began to go wrong when my marriage broke up' or 'Drink has made me go steadily downhill'. They may also validate other people's predictions: 'My wife always said I would end up in trouble if I didn't change my ways.' These explanations offer a mandate to diagnose, treat, and cast the offender in the socially sick role. But to ask for help is an admission of failure, and as Goffman says, the problem is that having admitted failure so little is actually done about it.

Social distance can also be preserved by the moral implications which underpin the rationale behind the expert's role. The literature on psycho-analysis and casework rarely considers that the theory may be harmful to the patients. In short it suggests that there are only degrees of good. The theory may be harmful if applied by non-experts, or it may be harmful if the wrong part of the theory is applied to a particular type of personality, i.e. an offender may not have the strength or ego development to cope with a certain level of intensity, but this does not mean the theory is defective. It means the reverse, that the defect lies in the patient who cannot receive the full treatment aid by definition, and has to be given less than was possible. Armed with such a secure idealist position it is no accident that experts believe they have something to offer everyone, and that everyone could benefit from their attention. They may have unlimited funds of goodness, but these will only be granted according to the experts' decision about the person's ability to accept it. To give, or to withhold, leads to a position of considerable power.

Although social distance is inherent in rehabilitation, simply because rehabilitation implies moral deficiencies, the practical application of social distance is social control.[8] In this context social control means a legitimate alteration of social roles, and social roles can be changed by overt methods or by subtle manipulation. Barbara Wootton calls these covert practices 'artificial tricks of friendliness' and implies that manipulation takes place whenever anyone seeks this type of professional help. Hadden, who is a lawyer, views with alarm the whole process of social control within the rehabilitative framework.

> The prevention of crime is not the ultimate aim of society. There are other values immeasurably more important, values which are enshrined in the rights of the individual within certain limits to live, to think, and to act as he wishes. The concept of treatment, if indiscriminately applied is in direct conflict with these rights. For the decision who is, and who is not a suitable case for treatment must in any given situation lie with some few persons, and their decision will be binding. The fact that they are supposedly acting for the benefit of the individual concerned is strictly irrelevant; the crucial point is that the rights of the individual have been merged in his assumed desire to be as the reformers wish him to be, and he is therefore no longer consulted.[9]

Hadden is concerned with the direct political implications of rehabilitation. He sees social control as being vested in the power of the treatment officials, which in this context means the ability to decide who is, and who is not to be treated. At a less direct political level C.S. Lewis is equally hostile to compulsory treatment. 'To be cured against one's will and to be cured of states which we may not regard as a disease is to be put on the level with those who have not yet reached the age of reason, or those who never will, to be classed with infants, imbeciles and domestic animals.'[10] Lewis's position is religious and moral but his argument is ideological when he says he has no wish to be remade after some pattern of normality, hatched, as he says, in a Viennese laboratory according to a doctrine to which he never professed allegiance. The rhetoric is emotive but this should not detract from the strength of his argument.

Lewis's point is not dissimilar to Joseph Gusfield's version of the enemy deviant who is regarded as an enemy, not because of the quality of his acts, but because of his hostility to basic norms.[11] The enemy deviant stands in contrast to the cynical deviant who may have committed more serious infractions but is self-seeking rather than ideologically hostile to the normative structure. The cynical deviant is regarded as a management problem and is not regarded as a threat whereas the enemy deviant is certainly a threat and requires swift and certain punishment.

Gusfield, however, takes the point further and provides an added twist to the social control argument. Included in his typology is the sick deviant, and the sick deviant is one who is regarded as not quite responsible for his actions and therefore should not be regarded as rational. Once classified as sick it no longer becomes necessary to take seriously anything he has to say but see it all as a symptom of his sickness. Complaints against the police are then seen as manifestations of paranoia, and long spells of unemployment merely reflect 'a workshy and inadequate personality'. Having once been regarded as sick, credibility is always likely to be weakened. The ex-mental patient for example would be regarded as having a relapse if he complained about his psychiatrist, but the integrity of the psychiatrist would of course still be preserved once it was seen as being a fabrication or manifestation of the patient's illness. A designation of sickness neutralizes complaints about institutions as well as confirming any suspicions that the offender or patient was really unstable. Social control agents are then in the fortunate position of having their cake and the halfpenny — a singularly rare occurrence — whereas the patient or offender ends up with neither.

One other critic, Isaiah Berlin, adopts a political stance and sees the whole process of interpreting behaviour as a threat to liberty,[12] because interpretations are a way of bypassing complaints about institutions and locating the problem in the personality of the complainant. How often this occurs is difficult to say but at a more sociological level interpretation can permit social control agents to acquire enormous power as long as they are able to see problems as primarily belonging to the patient. Treatment officials extensively use interpretation as part of their treatment talk and this puts them in a particularly favourable position to exert controls.

Although the social control argument is an important element in any analysis of the experts' treatment plans, in practice it operates rarely. Potentially it still remains a force to be considered but is minimized because contact between the offender and treatment officials is relatively infrequent. Social control, of course, remains and operates at two levels, first at the point where treatment is devised *for* the offender, and second, at the point where the offender's behaviour can be interpreted as symptomatic of his sickness. However, it operates mainly at a fairly low key level, and is usually brought out when it is necessary to maintain contact with an offender who is on probation, or detain someone in a mental hospital. For supporters of rehabilitation it is a sad but oft quoted fact that once on probation or in a mental hospital an offender will find that for the most part very little else actually happens. Treatment talk takes place relatively infrequently, and certainly at sufficiently rare intervals to doubt whether it can be effective in changing anyone's world view.

Supporters of rehabilitation accept the point that contacts are infrequent but usually suggest that treatment officials are grossly overworked. The lack of trained personnel is seen as the basis for most of the failures. In fact this is an over-simplified picture for although the trained personnel argument is sound at one level, the career structure and the bureaucratization mentioned in chapter 3 tend to push the personnel away from involvement with clients toward other success goals as measured by bureaucratic values. Are the personnel grossly overworked? An examination of the senior probation officer's role provides an important clue here, for the SPO's role is one of the few that has been given attention in recent years.

Most of the literature of the 1960s about the probation service contained references to the way in which the probation service was 'grossly overworked'. It was never clear if this meant that *all* probation officers, including supervisory grades, were grossly overworked, or only the basic grade officer. The ratio between supervisory grades and basic grade officers in 1972 was 4.5: 1.[13] Normally only the senior probation officer carries a caseload; other supervisory grades are employed in wholly administrative duties. The senior probation officer's caseload will be about ten cases, so in fact the bulk of the probation service's contact with clients will be by the basic grade officers. It seems pertinent to ask what these supervisory grades actually do. Obviously there are numerous outside duties involving public relations and contact with penal institutions but these, plus office administration, cannot account for all the working time. As far as the senior probation officers are concerned Jarvis says, 'A principal function of a senior is to offer regular casework supervision to his officers in his group.' The usual ratio of seniors to basic grade officers is 1:5.[14] In terms of man hours this means that if each officer was seen for two hours each week, supervisory sessions would only take 25 per cent of the time, leaving 50 per cent or 20 hours per week for administration to administer an office of five probation officers, and 10 hours for their caseload.

Supervisory sessions therefore appear to account for most of the senior probation officer's time. But what do these consist of? They begin typically with a reading of the basic grade probation officer's records, and then the direction of the session is switched to the probation officer's own psyche. Arthur Miles's study of probation supervisory sessions shows that senior probation officers did not rely on the officer's records as a basis for supervision. 'They often said they did . . . but they did not. Supervisors used the records primarily to alert themselves to problems . . . and for the details of the casework process the supervisors depended almost entirely upon personal discussion with workers.'[15] The functions of supervisory sessions and the methods of supervision are explained in 'Standards and Guides for Adult Probation'.

> Through supervision the officer is helped to recognise his own prejudices and biases which are reducing his helpfulness to his probationers . . . . Supervision is most imperative for officers whose casework skills are not fully developed and who are not yet qualified to proceed independently. Supervision is necessary also for experienced officers to help them maintain their skills and continue to improve their performance *and gain new insight.*[16] (Italics mine.)

Some supervision is of course necessary particularly with inexperienced officers, but why so much? For a service described as grossly overworked it is curious that senior probation officers should have so few cases, and spend so much time supervising basic grade officers who carry most of the contact with the clients.

The basic grade officer is trapped in the same dilemma, for he has to produce his records for the supervision session as well as for other administrative purposes. The volume of written work in probation records is truly amazing. Almost every interview is fully recorded with impressions and insights added. Every three months a summary is required of treatment and progress, and every telephone conversation related to each case is also recorded, again with impressions and insights, as is every letter and subsequent court appearance. Record keeping alone takes up to about 30 per cent of the probation officer's time. Add to this the secretary's time for shorthand and typing and the whole exercise becomes an expensive and costly business. Yet having devoted so much time to record keeping, the tragedy is that they are hardly ever read. High level supervisory grades might read them during an inspection of basic grade officer's work, and lower supervisory grades during some part of supervision, but that is about all. Apart from a few isolated instances basic grade officers rarely use them, whether it be to evaluate their own work or when a case is transferred to them by another officer. Probation officers say they prefer to make up their own minds about each client rather than rely on a colleague's judgment, which says little for their colleagues.

In spite of some official attempts to reduce the time spent on record keeping, probation records are still as copious and extensive as ever.

Some recalcitrant officers rebel but they are small in number. Others tend to keep three or six months behind with their record keeping and so expect to remember intricate details of an interview that could have taken place six months ago. Some deliberately keep their records in arrears; this they suggest 'helps with their predictions' as it then becomes possible to appear to have predictive abilities if one knows what has already happened. Knowing how records are prepared it is no wonder that probation officers rarely use them, but it is also curious that they still devote so much time to writing them.

Records within the probation service then tend to have little validity, particularly those prepared some months after the event. Of itself this would not matter except that they have an authority about them and a permanency.[17] They can be used as official documents, and are suddenly produced if, say, an offender has a subsequent court appearance. Probation officers in these circumstances would then tend to quote from their records in court as if they were authoritative documents. Whether the offender knew that his contacts with the probation service would be recorded in such minute detail is another matter. Perhaps if he did he would not be so forthcoming. Unless he was able to take his own notes of the interview it is clear that he is in a position of considerable disadvantage. The probation officer is armed with his records which provide his version and his truncated account of what happened[18] and the offender has nothing except his own memory which could be easily regarded as less reliable than the probation records.

Given the amount of time devoted to record keeping and to supervision, it is no surprise to find that the experts — in this instance the probation officers — spend so little time with their clients. Martin Davies and Andrea Knopf, with their particular sample show that probation officers spend about the same time on record keeping and administration as with the people they are expected to help. Excluding time spent on social enquiry reports, probation officers spent 23 per cent of their time on record keeping and administration compared with 25 per cent on home visits and office interviews.[19] Probation officers worked on average a 42 hour week (41 hours 23 minutes to be exact), which means that about 10.5 hours per week was actually spent in contact with clients. Assume that each probation officer has a caseload of fifty then each offender gets on average 12.6 minutes of probation officer's time per week, or just over three-quarters of an hour per month, or about 11 hours per year.

The lack of any substantial contact between probation officer and offender is now well known. In the USA Lewis Diana found similar results to those of Davies and Knopf, and was prompted to ask the question, 'Is probation necessary?' He concluded that it probably was not. In fact research findings have generally done little to support these experts' contention that most of the problems would be solved with better staff/client ratios. The evidence, however, does not support this argument.

The experts in probation have consistently argued that success rates have been depleted by high caseloads and by consistent and persistent changes in probation officers. The argument is plausible given their particular theoretical model. Emotional changes or changes in values, or changes in the offenders' world view, would be restricted if there was little time available with each client, and if the relationship was broken by changes in probation officers. Research results do not support these contentions. Richard Sparks in a review of the effectiveness of probation[20] discusses some of the research findings and suggests that 'at first sight it may seem surprising that anybody ever succeeds on probation at all'. On the question of size of caseloads Pye et al. pointed out that although workloads dropped in the probation service by 16 per cent between 1956 and 1960, there was no change in the overall success rate.[21] Martin Davies found similar results in Britain.[22] Lohman et al. found no significant differences in their success rates of offenders who were randomly allocated to intensive and minimum supervision. 'Intensive supervision' meant the officer (in this case the parole officer) had 25 cases and 6.71 contacts per month, whilst 'minimum' meant case loads of up to 125 with 0.48 contacts per month. What was additionally galling was that no one with a successful outcome and with intensive supervision listed the treatment officer as being a significant factor in their success. They attributed their success to their own perceived non-criminal orientation and to assistance from family and friends. Finally the SIPU (Special Intensive Parole Unit) study in California found that a general reduction in caseloads and a corresponding increase in contacts had no affect on overall success rates.[23] As regards changes in probation officers Martin Davies and Brenda Chapman also found that overall success rates were not affected by these changes.[24]

It must be remembered that these are not isolated studies carefully selected to show that probation ideals are as yet unproven, but that almost all studies show the same results with the same monotonous regularity. They point to the very obvious conclusion that this method of rehabilitating offenders fails to live up to its claims. It fails in another sense too, for when probation is compared with other forms of penal 'treatment' — particularly that having no claim to rehabilitation — it simply does no better. If anything it fares slightly worse, when compared to the fine, and no better than a conditional discharge.[25] Its main advantage over prison is that it is less costly, but on an economic basis is still more costly than the fine, particularly if the fine is collected.

Quite clearly, some offenders *do* benefit from being on probation, although even this statement is still largely unsupported by research findings; we can only assume that this should be so or at least put it negatively and say it is doubtful if many are adversely affected. But if probation officers do not appear to succeed all that well, what about the psychiatrists. Do they fare any better? They, after all, act as advisers, and are role models for probation officers. Yet for all their alleged expertise psychiatrists appear to be no more successful than the probation officers in treating criminals. In perhaps the only study which could compare the two groups of experts, Max Grunhut found that psychiatric treatment did no better than other non-expert measures.[26] Grunhut's research was concerned with studying offenders placed on probation with a condition of psychiatric treatment. He found that the results resembled those of ordinary penal measures, i.e. that men were more likely to be reconvicted than women, and those with previous convictions were more likely to be reconvicted than first offenders. Grunhut's most revealing conclusion was that there was no evidence that offenders who had failed to respond to ordinary penal measures responded to psychiatric ones.

Grunhut's research is important in another respect, for it illustrates the tensions between the psychiatrists operating a rehabilitative model of penal treatment and the courts. Offenders on probation with a condition of psychiatric treatment break the conditions of their order if they discontinue treatment without the approval of the psychiatrist. This can mean either absconding from the hospital if they are in-patients, or failing to attend the clinics if they are out-patients. Grunhut found that about 1 in 4 of his sample left hospital without permission, but were rarely brought back to court on a breach of requirements of their probation order. Furthermore the liaison probation officer was rarely told that the offender had absconded, nor indeed were the courts. It appears as if the psychiatrists operated as if some legal rules did not exist, and they certainly acted with a lofty disdain toward the probation service. Why, then, were the courts not told? No doubt it was partly because of the additional administrative work required but also because the psychiatrist did not think that a return to court would, as they often say, 'do the offender any good'. Implicit in this phrase is a belief that they, the psychiatrists, know what is good for the offenders, and they do not believe that the penal system as it is currently constructed operates in the offenders' best interests. Such a view places the expert on a higher plane than the democratic process of the rule of law, and there is a further assumption that they, the experts, operate the legal rules when and if they think fit. Goffman once noted that it was an odd historical fact that persons concerned with promoting civil liberties in other areas of life tended to favour giving the psychiatrist complete discretionary power over the patient. He added that patients, to his knowledge, had not been polled in this matter.[27] Neither apparently have the courts.

Do psychiatrists fare any better with offender patients sent to them under the Mental Health Acts? Apparently not, nor do they seem to abide more by the legal rules than they do for Section 4 probation admissions. Offenders who are kept in normal mental hospitals as opposed to the special hospitals like Rampton or Broadmoor tend if anything to get released fairly quickly. In one of the few studies on the length of time spent in hospital Dr Rollin found that 65 per cent of his sample on Section 60 hospital orders left hospital within six months, 32 per cent within three months, and 7 out of the 9 of his sample on Section 4 also left within six months.[28] A large number seemed to have absconded rather than been discharged after completion of treatment. Nigel Walker and Sarah McCabe, in their large-scale study of offender patients also note the high rate of absconding, a method which they describe as a simpler and more popular road to freedom.

> Absconding was common amongst unrestricted offender patients in ordinary hospitals, especially amongst schizophrenics and psychopaths of whom 1 in 7 absconded during their first year. There were even 5 restricted offender patients who managed to abscond in their first year, a fact which emphasises that a restriction order is no guarantee of secure custody.[29]

Only a minority were kept in locked wards (37 per cent), a point which led Walker and McCabe to suggest that the receiving hospitals could not have appreciated the danger of the offender patients. Similarly Rollin, who was Deputy Superintendent of the Hospital from which he took the sample, also said that 'I have no doubt that to a charge of custodial inefficiency entered against Horton hospital, a verdict of "guilty" will be returned.' There is nothing new here, absconding has been going on for years, the only point worth making about it is that courts still keep sending offenders to such institutions apparently oblivious to the fact that so few stay long enough to get treatment.

On the other hand it also appears that not much treatment would have been given had they have stayed. Walker and McCabe make the point forcibly: 'We were struck by the fact that where information was given the three most frequently mentioned forms (of treatment) apart from drugs were non-medical; that is of kinds usually left to occupational therapists and nursing staff.'[30]

The most common form of treatment was 'occupational therapy' (45 per cent of the cases) followed by 'habit training' and 'supervision'

(35 per cent). Psychotherapy was mentioned in 25 per cent of the cases and group therapy in 5 per cent. Contact then with the treatment officials was rare, most of the time being spent on occupational therapy. Walker and McCabe note that the same could be said for prisons — although the term used in that case is work — but they raise the question about the nature of this occupational therapy. 'What is interesting to the detached observer is the intense criticism to which prison work is subjected and the comparative rarity of any critical examination of occupational therapy.'[31]

Walker and McCabe's study is the most comprehensive piece of research on the efficacy of hospital treatment in Britain. The results show that hospital treatment is no better or worse than other forms of penal 'treatment', as only a little over a third of the men in their sample, and rather less than half of the women, succeeded in keeping out of the criminal courts or mental hospitals during their two year follow up. They called their cohort a stage army because of the way it moved from one institution to another: 'To call it a stage army is to some extent justified by the frequent entrances which most of its members made either by way of prison gates or through the revolving doors of the mental hospitals.'[32]

Yet in a curious way it is unfair to compare hospitals with prisons, for hospitals have the obvious advantage of being able to choose the offenders they are prepared to treat. Apart from special hospitals such as Rampton and Broadmoor, a court, before it can make a hospital order, requires agreement from the hospital that they are willing to admit the patient. Prisons have no such choice. Probation, too, offers a method of selection, for the probation officers invariably suggest to the courts who should, or who should not, be placed on probation and the courts invariably agree. No other branches of the penal system are able to choose their clients in this way and it does suggest that the experts have a built-in advantage to begin with. That they are no more successful is either a reflection of their expertise, or of the offenders they choose, or both. Either way, no one should be misled into thinking that they take the more difficult cases, or that prisons take sane offenders whilst the experts have the insane. It is possible that prisons have numerically more offenders who are 'mentally ill' than do the hospitals, and they cannot choose or preselect them.

If experts have not been all that successful in treating offenders, perhaps in other areas they could be more successful? Allocation procedures, for example, are essential to rehabilitationist philosophies, for they are the vehicle by which rehabilitation could be operational- ized. The remainder of this chapter will be devoted to allocation pro- cedures, for they offer some important features of rehabilitation which require additional emphasis. Allocation procedures, then, on the face of it, would offer a particularly good example of the experts in operation.

Experts see the ever increasing crime rate as a failure of deterrent/retributive philosophies. They suggest that punitive philosophies are a failure because of the narrow definition of crime, and are convinced that their own reformist view is wider and likely to be more effective. In fact some measure of autonomy has been given to the experts — allocation procedures being a good example. None the less, a reformist would still argue that the present method of sentencing produces too much inflexibility. By this they mean that an offender can be sentenced to prison and only be released at the time allocated by the court, although he may be ready for release much earlier. A longer period in prison might only make matters worse. In short, rehabilitationists want flexibility, and above all want a more expert method of diagnosis followed by allocation procedures designed to meet each offender's personal needs. This all adds up to either more experts, or to more sophisticated methods of diagnosis, or both. It also takes us back to that area of rehabilitation which attempts to fit the offender to a specified form of treatment. There are a number of difficulties with this approach, mainly centring round the question of diagnosis, and which are best illustrated by examining the current methods of allocation.

The first problem centres around the question of diagnosing sentences at the pre-sentence stage. Consider first the theoretical problems involved.

In a very real sense it has always been accepted that probation officers have on their caseloads what they call 'dead wood' and which means in practice that there is a percentage of their caseload who do not require much contact with the probation officer. Conversely there are many offenders in prison who could be as effectively dealt with by a probation order — or put another way, do not require imprisonment. Current research on the efficacy of penal sanctions suggests that for many offenders it does not really matter what sentence is given. For others, it may only be a matter of deciding between custodial and non-custodial sanctions. Nigel Walker suggests that it is logically — and empirically — possible to see offenders as belonging to any one of a number of different groups:

1 Those who will go straight whatever the sentence.
2 Those who will not go straight whatever the sentence.
3 Those who will go straight if given a certain sentence but not any of the others.
4 Those who will go straight if given one or two sentences but not the others;
5 and so on, until the group is reached for who there is only one ineffective sentence.[33]

Viewed in this way penal sanctions are not separate or discrete alternatives. There may be a few offenders who fall into category 3 of Walker's typology and there may be others who would require custodial as opposed to non-custodial sentences, but those falling into category 3 may not be numerically large, and certainly no larger than those falling into other categories.

Whereas Walker sees penal measures as largely interchangeable, supporters of the rehabilitative ideal see penal sanctions as being specific to the needs of an offender. Nigel Walker calls this approach the 'diagnostic fallacy', for it assumes that only one penal measure is suitable for that particular offender. He rightly points out that the diagnostic argument is fallacious because the limited range of penal measures precludes any systematic attempt to operate the model except in a very general way. Assuming that each offender has different needs it is hardly systematic to fit a variety of offenders into four or five penal sanctions. Walker thinks that it is logically possible, given his model, to sentence some offenders to a whole range of penal sanctions, from a conditional discharge, to imprisonment, to a hospital order, and future success would not be affected.

Sentencing according to a diagnostic approach is also likely to be fallacious because to operate the model successfully the penal sanctions must function in an anticipated way. This means that when a diagnosis is made and a certain course of treatment prescribed that treatment should not operate in a random or haphazard manner. Unfortunately for the rehabilitationists the penal system is often haphazard. An offender might 'need' to be fined, so the court imposes the fine but the offender never pays, and the fine may be written off. (This is by no means unusual.) In this sense he never receives his treatment but there is nothing to suggest from the reconviction rates that failure to pay a fine is less successful than for those conscientious enough to pay it. The penal system does not operate like a general hospital, or even like an idealized version of a general hospital, and there are no sets of routine instructions nor standards to be uniformly applied. Neither can there ever be, when decisions to invoke legal sanctions are dependent on individual sanctions often underscored by individual moralities. For example, the Court of Appeal conceded that the police have a very wide discretion in enforcing the law. The Chief Police Officer decides the manner in which that police force is to be deployed, whether enquiries should be instituted, and whether to prosecute in any particular case. The decision is not the Chief Officer's alone.[34] Some offences must be reported to the Director of Public Prosecutions who must decide whether the police can intervene. Certain regulations restrict the police powers, but within these limits discretion remains considerable. The Director of Public Prosecutions also has discretionary powers; he will only prosecute for example if a prosecution is 'in the public interest'. What could be less routine than this, and what could be further from the certain fixed and immutable world of modern science?

Arguments about diagnosis within the penal system must inevitably stand or fall on the answer to that penultimate question: Diagnosing what? If the answer is a social illness, a maladjustment or even a need, each reply poses its own intractable problem. The social pathology model is currently being questioned, having had considerable freedom over the last few decades, and with the questioning comes an added realization that 'diagnosis' remains in the words of Professor Flew, 'a conceptual shambles'.

Diagnosis takes place at a number of different points within the penal system. There is a form of diagnosis at the sentencing stage, as illustrated by social enquiry reports, but it is at the post-sentence stage that the major allocation procedures operate. Having arrived at a hospital, or a prison, another diagnosis is made (this can be called a second order diagnosis) and this is aimed at finding the right sort of institution to satisfy that offender's needs. Ideally, the second order diagnosis should be a continuation of the first, in the sense that it should be prepared by the same people who initially suggested that type of penal sanction. Only in mental hospitals is this likely to happen, when the psychiatrist responsible for the treatment would also be the psychiatrist who recommended hospitalization to the courts. In prisons a probation officer might have initially recommended imprisonment but would not be involved in the allocation procedure. The second order diagnosis is therefore usually made by a panel of experts who before making their decision would have collected all the relevant reports, including an up to date report on the offender's progress whilst in the allocation centre.

Allocation, based as it is on the diagnostic model, is at one level plausible, but on another level, deceptively simple. The aim is to allocate the offender to the right institution. Stated in this way it immediately becomes plausible. Gittens, who is an ardent exponent of allocation, argues, quite rightly, that allocation depends first on a method of classification, and that many forms of classification are accepted as common practice in other walks of life. In this sense, he suggests that the classification procedures used in the penal system are no different in principle to any other. Once offenders can be classified they can then be allocated.

The hospitals for instance have separate medical and surgical wards, special departments for children, out-patient clinics and distinct establishments for mental cases. In the Army recruits are sorted out at an early stage of their training and are drafted to units where their

different capacities may be best employed . . . . The work of
Education Authorities and Juvenile Employment Bureaux in
advising school leavers is aimed at providing young people with
interesting and suitable occupations and avoiding frustration and
unhappiness.[35]

Gittens is of course quite right. Long before the reformist argument
gained ground the penal system was operating a rudimentary classification procedure which still exists today. Children do not mix with
adult offenders, and men do not mix with women offenders. Some
prisons are for long term offenders, others take only short sentences;
whilst all prisoners are categorized according to their potential risk
to society. In other words the prisoners have all been classified and
allocated to respective roles.

Yet Gittens's example is misleading, for it makes little sense to
talk of classificatory procedures without at the same time relating
these to the aims of these procedures. In Gittens's example hospital
classifications are used with different aims in mind than those for the
army and education authorities. With the penal system at present
there are a number of classificatory procedures all having different
aims. For example, the initial classification of sex was presumably
aimed at denying sexual contact and was to be part of the punishment,
whilst the aim of the age classification was to protect the young from
criminal contamination. Gittens really walks around this issue and
does not stipulate that the classificatory system he advocates is
aimed at assisting with the process of rehabilitation. It is also important
to note the additonal conceptual confusion that exists in most of
this part of the rehabilitationist literature. Terms like 'classification'
and 'allocation' are used interchangeably whereas they are analytically
separate; i.e. the one precedes the other. Gittens is really arguing for
a classificatory system, in order that an allocation system can operate
later, but this is not always clear.

The first task then is to classify the offenders. In line with the
rehabilitative ideal this means identifying their needs. Here lies the
first difficulty, for what are these needs? Is there a difference between
a need and a want? What criteria are there to be used to identify a
need? These questions have rarely been asked, but as we shall see when
when we examine the classificatory and allocation processes they
are extremely important.

Ideally the system should operate with the experts being able to
make their diagnosis on the basis of a large amount of evidence on
the offender, and then on the basis of additional evidence allocate the
offender to the appropriate institution. For the moment ignore the
organizational demands within the allocation system and ignore the

organizational restraints in the appropriate institution, i.e. assume the
experts have an unlimited amount of time to spend on each case, and
assume that all institutions have places available to take each offender.
How then are decisions made? There are of course certain reliable
factors such as age, sex, previous convictions and IQ, but experts
need more than this if they are to assess 'needs'. Gittens certainly
wants 'something else' as he calls it and this 'something else' turns
out to be a complex of factors involving attitudes to life,
temperamental types, motivating forces, and the 'effects that
adversity has produced and does produce'.[36] This 'something else'
is nothing if not a multi-dimensional concept.

Having teased out the complex of factors, Gittens then develops a
typology which he calls a typology of responses. It contains four
categories.

A.	Positive	This describes a boy who tends to make his own decisions. They may be good or bad but he moves, as it were, under his own steam.
B.	Confused	Many of our boys (Gittens is concerned here with approved school boys) lack stability or direction, and their efforts to achieve their goals, which may or may not be socially or morally desirable, are not tenacious.
C.	Apathetic	Many of our boys seem to be totally lacking or nearly so in drive, interests or initiative.
D.	Psychopathic	The term is not used in its strict psychological meaning but describes those boys many of whose actions seem to lie outside the power of their conscious control. They need special therapy.

These responses are not discrete alternatives for it is possible that an
offender could be a positive, confused (vaguely) apathetic psychopath.
Nor are they value free. They are also vague, which at best produces
flexibility, but functionally the lack of clarity permits the intrusion of
the experts' own intuitive clinical variables. Note also the headings to
the four responses, each in their way, apart from A, offering a form of
denunciation. Although Gittens was concerned with approved school
boys the system as it currently operates in borstals appears to operate
against a similar background of vagueness. R.L. Morrison has graphically described the way in which borstal allocation seems to operate.

I would regard the judgement process in allocation as wherever
possible intuitive, global, and concrete with a reluctance to take
matters further where there is clear agreement about disposal and a
resort to analysis of a more or less disciplined kind only when this is

clearly made necessary by differences of opinion, apparent discrepancies of fact, ambiguities, and inconsistencies arising from a lad's behaviour and so on.[37]

Morrison is no novice and no casual observer at allocation procedures. He has had considerable experience at borstal allocation and for that reason alone his arguments should be taken seriously. To Morrison, allocation procedures typically begin with consideration of what he calls 'general reference points' such as age, previous convictions, etc., followed by consideration of specific training needs such as educational attainment or some technical interest, followed by 'diffuse personal or psychological needs' regarded by Morrison as 'the heart of the matter'. These include the certain kinds of relationships thought to be required in the treatment programme, such as the framework of support as opposed to the rigours of the disciplined regime. Being 'the heart of the matter' it is no accident that these are the least tangible and the least scientific. This is what Morrison means when he describes the whole process as intuitive and global.

Morrison is optimistic about the future of allocation procedures, but he holds out no hope for large scale changes in the immediate future. He sums up the present position in these terms:

> Current Borstal allocation methods are as sensitive and discriminating as are required or allowed by our present state of knowledge of exactly what happens in the training field. Improvements in allocation must await much greater knowledge especially of the interpersonal dynamics of the training process. This is likely to be a slow process.[38]

There is another limitation too. In order to operate the model successfully some detailed knowledge must be available about the type of regime to which the offender could be allocated. In medicine, which is the model the experts favour, no one claiming expertise in broken legs would suggest the patient should attend a clinic where there may be only a vague knowledge about broken legs. Or if there was a wide knowledge, then that particular expert would want to know if it was being utilized. Yet the treatment experts do not appear to concern themselves about such rudimentary information. Knowledge about a particular institution may be fragmentary, or it may be biased; it rarely, according to R.M. Fisher, appears detailed.

> We send them to institutions which we know only from having spent some time there in the past, from the service grapevine, from the label which the institution has selected for itself, or from the

description of what the institution is doing by those persons, members of the management ranks of the institution who are not necessarily in an advantageous position for evaluating what the institution is doing.[39]

So, even if the method of assessment was efficient the allocation procedure would be defective at the point where decisions are made about the institution. Yet how could it be otherwise? Institutions are not static entities, and no panel of experts could have special and intimate knowledge of each institution. Descriptions of penal institutions must of necessity be broad and perhaps even idealized so that an institution claiming specialization in, for example, certain types of trade training, may simply be making a claim for recognition rather than an honest appraisal of the situation.

But there is an even greater problem which relates to the issues raised in chapter 2 about the rehabilitationists' conception of crime. Classification and allocation, as described by Gittens and Morrison, is not really about crime but about behaviour. Gittens's types of response do not explain why these certain characteristics lead to crime rather than, say suicide, or any other type of deviant behaviour, or indeed why they lead to deviance at all. There must be countless people in Britain having those particular responses who are in no sense deviant, let alone criminal. The 'diffuse personal and psychological needs' described by Morrison may well exist among criminals and among non-criminals alike, and since the penal system is about stopping further offences, it seems that some recognition of the notion of crime, as opposed to behaviour, is required. Unless, or until, experts include the concept of crime into their theoretical framework deficiencies will continue to exist.

Apart from these theoretical issues allocation methods have highlighted an important practical issue which, like the studies on efficacy of probation and hospitalization, illustrate the difference between what the experts claim to be doing and what they actually achieve. Such a difference, unhappily for the experts, pervades the whole area of their province whether it be at the level of diagnosis or of treatment. In view of their lack of pronounced success it is even more astounding that their influence should have become so profound. Expertise, however, does not operate in a vacuum but requires support from other subgroups some of whom need to be primarily at a practical level, as in the case of other social workers — and some at a more ideological level. As far as the latter is concerned support had long been forthcoming from criminology and the criminologists themselves. Criminologists had until recently adopted the experts' world view and accepted their intellectual demands. This is why Stan Cohen complained that the only journal dealing with crime in Britain, the 'British Journal of Criminology', was dominated by clinical papers written by psychiatrists, social workers and practitioners. He meant by this that the clinical experts called the criminological tune.

Now of course there is nothing of itself wrong with a clinical view, and clinicians in criminology have a right to their point of view as has anyone else. What was wrong was that the clinical view was overpowering and it stifled discussion. Experts are concerned with causes, and in particular with causal factors, and as part of their task want to identify factors which would help with their treatment plans. Criminologists try to provide these, so British criminology became identified either with a kind of factor theory, or with preventative measures which in practice meant prediction studies. Some criminologists have now turned their attentions elsewhere because of the sterility of this approach.

It is only possible to speculate why criminologists played into the clinicians' demands. Stan Cohen sees the whole area of criminology as tied to state influence by research grants and by an inherent pragmatism in British intellectual life. He thinks criminologists are seen as intellectual experts whose function is to do the state's bidding, and the experts' bidding too. Pragmatism then becomes closely allied to support of the status quo.

Yet the defects of the rehabilitationists' argument were plain. There was little in the research findings which would support the basic contention that differences existed in a qualitative sense between people who did and who did not break social rules. No research was ever able to show that there were special personality defects which were peculiar to criminals, whilst most research concerned with isolating criminogenic factors simply contradicted other research in that field. Consider the case of drug addiction. Alfred Lindesmith collected a list of thirty-three different terms, all of which had been used to describe the personality of the drug taker. Since the list contained terms such as 'passive psychopath', 'hostile', 'weak','paranoid' and 'essentially normal', Lindesmith's conclusion was that this type of research had little to offer any basic theory of drug addiction. Yet still the research workers persisted, adding to the list but somehow never reaching any firm conclusions which would produce that elusive difference.

Experts claim that more research is needed. Evidence to the Royal Commission on the Penal System is full of demands for more research the purpose being to probe further the workings of the criminal mind or to examine the criminals' social backgrounds. Yet for all those countless studies, each in its own way producing a special piece of statistical information, they have all what Stan Cohen calls 'a depressing sameness about them'. Furthermore, and here is the paradox, experts rarely use that research information anyway. A journal such as 'Social Work Today' occasionally harangues its readers about not keeping up to date with research findings. The lack of interest may not be due to the quality of the studies nor because social workers rarely find them worth reading, but perhaps because there really is a depressing sameness about them. Does it really make very much difference to a practitioner to know that X per cent were divorced or that X per cent came from a broken home and Y per cent were neurotic. Experts have not time for such statistical information for it hardly helps them when faced in their office with a client just released from prison. The prediction studies for borstal shared the same fate, for when told that A had a 90 per cent chance of success probation officers rightly asked if they could then be told whether it meant that A was in the 90 per cent category or the 10 per cent. For all Stan Cohen's criticism about traditional research being geared up to the experts' theoretical approach, that research offered few practical benefits.

Throughout this and the preceding chapter, I have tried to show that the defect in the current approach has been in terms of measurable success and of failing to produce the goods. This failure, however, is not created by a shortage of experts but is a failure of their theories of crime. In the next two chapters I want to expand some of these points and examine some other areas which are similarly defective. The subjects to be examined are social enquiry reports and rehabilitation within penal institutions. Both areas will pick up and extend some of the points in this chapter; the section on social enquiry reports, for example, extends the discussions on diagnosis, and the chapter on penal institutions picks up some of these same arguments and continues with the points raised about allocation.

5

Sentencing and the social enquiry report

Earlier chapters were concerned with relating rehabilitation to social pathology and to examining the effects of this model. In this and the next two chapters the rehabilitative ideal will be examined as it currently operates within the penal system. In this chapter special attention will be given to the sentencing process, for it is here that the major conflicts about rehabilitation often take place. The courts — along with the police and prison officals — have traditionally become the main targets for attack, being characterized as essentially punitive and as sentencing according to outmoded principles. In their evidence to the Royal Commission on the Penal System the Association of Psychiatric Social Workers argued that adult courts are passing sentences without sufficient psychiatric information, whilst the Fabian Society was convinced of the sterility of the punitive-retributive attitude which still prevails in too many of our adult courts. The British Psychological Society put the matter more succinctly when it said that the sentencing policies of the courts exercise a considerable influence upon the penal system by determining which category of penal treatment an offender shall be allocated.[1] The problem of classification is therefore central to the whole field of penological research because only then can there 'be improvements in methods of sentencing and allocation'. The courts provide the input into the penal system. The rehabilitative ideal requires those inputs to be classified, but classified in such a way as to fit the 'needs' of the offender to the treatment facilities. 'Needs' would of course be determined by that ideology, hence the comments of the Association of Psychiatric Social Workers that courts are passing sentence without sufficient psychiatric information.

90

In short, the proponents of the rehabilitative ideal require sentences to be individualized. Again, the term is deceptively simple, for what does 'individualized' mean? Presumably it is not related to offences, nor to a standard set of variables which courts should consider before passing sentence, and which Roger Hood called 'equality of considerations'. 'Individualized' in this context means being concerned with the offender's personal and social history where the offence is only one factor and no more important than the psycho-social ones. David Matza describes individualized justice as follows:

> Spokesmen for individualized justice do not suggest that offence is irrelevant, rather that it is one of the many considerations that are to be used in arriving at a sound disposition. Offence like many other forms of behaviour is to be taken as an indication or symptom of the [offender's] personal and social disorder. The principles of individualized justice suggest that disposition is to be guided by a full understanding of the client's personal and social character and by his individual needs. This view is well captured by the slogan which suggests that nowadays the treatment fits the individual whereas in olden days the punishment fitted the crime.[2]

Matza's account captures the essence of individualized justice. He also points to a number of additional problems. The first is to decide which social and personal characteristics are the relevant ones. Alternatively everything may be relevant. In one sense everything must be relevant but as no court can consider *all* the factors some selection must take place and some factors will be considered more relevant than others. It is then a question of deciding which factors are the most relevant and which can be left out. When that question is settled the next one appears: perhaps some factors are not only more relevant than others but if we are involved in a scientific exercise, some ought to be given more weight. Psychic development, for example, could be seen as more important than social characteristics. Once that is agreed there is still the residual problem of who is to make these decisions.

Matza sees the whole process of individualized sentencing as a 'mystification', and a form of mystification unsurpassed in any other area of modern society. In this he is surely right, for since courts have an acknowledged difficulty in deciding whether an offence has been committed at all, how much more mystifying it is to make them decide about the 'needs' of an offender. In practice, however, these issues are rarely discussed. What happens is that a certain standard set of 'relevant' factors become imbued with some meaning, and this is routinely presented as a form of individualized justice. Social enquiry reports for example typically concentrate on a set of home circumstances and psychic features of the offender and these are weighted according to the theoretical orientations of the report writer.

There have been numerous attempts to introduce a more individualized sentencing practice in British courts. The most radical proposal involved the introduction of sentencing panels. Had these proposals been accepted they would have removed from the courts the power to pass sentence and the power would have been given to a group of experts. A modified version of sentencing panels already exists in the juvenile courts as the 1969 Act has reduced the power of magistrates to impose specific sentences when they make a care order. When a care order has been made, social workers have the power to decide whether the child should remain in a penal institution or go home. Flexibility of treatment has replaced the traditional view that only the courts could say whether a juvenile should remain in an institution. So far there has been no real attempt to extend these provisions to the adult courts.

The argument for sentencing panels was persuasive, even if unpractical. Professor Glueck was an ardent advocate of panels. He wanted 'a skilled administrative board, specially qualified . . . for the work of *scientific* determination of the peno-correctional consequences of convictions'.[3] (Emphasis mine.) Notice the word 'scientific' and notice also the phrase 'a skilled administrative board'. Norval Morris took the argument a stage further. He listed four major features of modern sentencing, all of which explicitly undermine the courts' ability to pass the 'right' sentences. There are of course many variations on Morris's arguments, some of which appear in a less overt form, but Morris at least gives a clear exposition of his particular stance.

1. The individual personality of the judge or magistrate plays too large a part in the assessment of the punishment; for example, whether a given offender goes to gaol for a protracted retributive sentence or receives remedial treatment while living in the community often depends on the chance of which court happens to sentence him. There is in other words too great an illogical and fortuitous variation between sentences.
2. The Bench frequently lacks sufficient information and knowledge concerning the personality of the offender and the social group from which he comes to impose a rational sentence on him.
3. The Bench frequently lacks sufficient information and knowledge of the penal system which carries out its sentences and of the effects of different types of punishment on different types of offenders.
4. Generally judges and magistrates are insufficiently trained for the awesome task of imposing sentences on their fellow men and in particular they have shown themselves to be out of touch with the work and plans of other authorities concerned with the punishment

of criminals.[4]

Most of Morris's points are of course valid, particularly those raised in paragraph 4. There *are* disparities in sentencing, and the extent of these disparities is too wide to ignore.[5] Morris is right to draw attention to this but his argument is not about reforming existing procedures, he wants to replace them with the sentencing panel.

If one of the major reasons for introducing panels is to reduce disparities then Morris misses the point. As John Hogarth has shown in a very detailed study of sentencing practices in Ontario, sentencing is a very personal matter. Disparities may exist between courts, but each magistrate is highly consistent within his own pattern of sentencing. Some magistrates always send certain types of offenders to prison when others would always make a probation order, whilst others would always request a social enquiry report before passing that type of sentence. In short, magistrates were individually highly consistent, even if their consistency differed from that of their colleagues.[6]

Now there is no reason to suggest that sentencing panels would be any different. Disparities would still exist although each panel would be consistent, having its own pattern of sentencing. Moreover, to suggest that a panel of experts from different disciplines would reduce anomalies and somehow arrive at a uniform level of sentences is like suggesting that three or five magistrates from different backgrounds will also arrive at uniformity, or that the way to reduce disparities in courts is to broaden the social base of the judiciary. On the one hand the person with the highest status within a group tends to have the greatest influence on the normative structure; a process which operates in a way reminiscent of Howard Becker's hierarchy of credibility. The panel's values would emanate from him, particularly if he was chairman and the panel's values would therefore be institutionalized to the highest status member. Paradoxically a broader social base may have the overall effect of widening disparities rather than reducing them. Yet perhaps in a curious way disparities are peripheral to Morris's argument for he seems to be more concerned with questions of individualized justice than about variations in the present practice, and these are not necessarily the same thing.

The second and third paragraphs in Morris's statement will be considered later under the general question of the types of information presented to the courts. The second part of paragraph 4 is also manifestly true. Judges and magistrates *are* insufficiently trained. Having acknowledged this, the answer might appear to lie in a more detailed training programme, that is, if training is thought to be necessary. Yet Morris does not appear to want a better training programme, he wants a panel consisting of members who are not 'out of touch'. This leads back to the basic question of who should replace the 'out of touch' judges and magistrates. Presumably we are back to those 'experts' again.

Given that we know who these 'experts' are, then who will train them, or will they have acquired their expertise elsewhere? If not, then perhaps we need a panel of super-experts to act as instructors. But who are they? Certainly they are not to be found amongst criminologists, and certainly not amongst those who routinely work in the treatment bureaucracies. Furthermore, what would happen if there was an appeal against these experts' decisions? Again presumably there would be an appeal to those super-experts whose ability to diagnose 'needs' was considered greater than those at the sentencing panel level.

Not all arguments for sentencing panels would remove the courts' power to pass sentences. A suggestion by the Sub-Committee on Penal Reform of the Royal College of Physicians would want to leave some of the court machinery intact. The courts would decide whether a person should be given a custodial sentence or not, and if so then the panel would operate thereafter.

> The Court might for example authorize the *detention* of an individual for the protection of the community specifying the degree of security required, while leaving it to a panel of 'experts' subsequently to tailor the details of the individual programme. The qualifications of such 'experts' would be a matter for further discussion . . . .[7]

Certainly the qualifications of the panel ought to be a matter for discussion; more than that, they ought to be a matter of proven ability. In an earlier paragraph the Sub-Committee noted that in certain continental countries the opinion of an examining psychiatrist is treated with great respect, and the medical and psychiatric background of the offender is admitted in evidence and accepted by the court when it comes from authorized sources. When reading this passage it is difficult to avoid thinking that psychiatrists have shunned the mantle and status of the expert.

There are other problems with the treatment panels, although mainly of a practical nature. If panels were to work effectively there would need to be two phases of the sentencing process. The first would be the data collection phase. This would require interviews with offenders, followed by interviews with some 'significant others'. Given the present orientation toward individualized sentencing the 'significant others' would most likely be members of the family, employers, schoolteachers, etc. Then once the data had been collected, the experts would be assembled to decide on sentence. The trial incidentally would continue as before — the lawyer's legitimate right to try cases and give verdicts has rarely been disputed. After the trial the case would be handed over to the panel.

How many additional personnel would be required? In the first place if we cover all indictable offences then about 1¼ million social enquiry reports would be needed, or put another way, six times more than are being done at present.[8] Assuming that these reports would not be more time consuming than with the present method, and assuming that the outcome would not produce a significant increase in case-loads, it is likely the probation service would need to be increased by about 500 per cent. Bearing in mind that the probation service is not up to its full strength the prospect of introducing that part of the programme becomes slim.

Similar problems arise when we consider the sentencing panels themselves. Richard Sparks has estimated on the basis of 1963 figures that there were about a thousand magistrates' courts in England and Wales and a total of 476,100 persons of all ages were found guilty of indictable and non-indictable offences (excluding traffic). Even if tribunals were restricted to magistrates' courts that still leaves 200,000 offenders to be sentenced by such bodies each year.

Let us assume that each tribunal could deal with offenders at an average rate of one per hour, eight hours a day for 260 working days a year. This assumption is probably extremely optimistic but never mind. For even if we make it, nearly 100 treatment tribunals would be required to deal with the total number of persons of all ages now convicted of indictable offences in magistrates courts. Now who is going to run these 100 tribunals? Precisely where are we to find 100 psychiatrists who are both competent and willing to spend all of their time dealing with convicted offenders — at a time when for example the Prison Medical Service is desperately short of persons with psychiatric training? Where are we to find 100 psychologists, sociologists and educators both competent and willing to sit full time on sentencing tribunals? Plainly we are not. At present it would probably be difficult to find the persons needed to staff the dozen or so tribunals which would be needed . . . to deal with persons now convicted at [Higher] Courts; it is simply absurd to suppose that eight times as many 'experts' could be found at anytime within the forseeable future to deal with all of these persons convicted of similar offences at Magistrates' Courts.[9]

Sparks goes on to say that the complete transfer of sentencing to tribunals is pure utopianism and the sooner it is forgotten the better. However, Nigel Walker believes that the strength of the tribunal argument has been weakened by proposing that *every* sentence should be dealt with by tribunals.[10] He wants to limit it to cases where the courts want to place offenders on probation or be given a custodial sentence first, with the prospect of later release under supervision.[11] On Sparks's figures, i.e. that one tribunal is capable of sentencing 2,080 people per year, we would still need a large number of tribunals.

Richard Sparks's plea for forgetting about sentencing panels has not been accepted, although the argument has shifted in recent years. The new approach wants to retain the courts but it dilutes their power by introducing other groups supposedly more qualified in sentencing techniques. The aim is to establish a 'partnership in sentencing'.[12] The partners would be the courts on one side, and the probation service, local authority social workers and psychiatrists on the other. Yet it is difficult to see how such a partnership would work. Would it be an *equal* partnership with all parties having equal status? If not, who would be the dominant partner? In the event of an appeal, would the partnership continue or would partnership only exist at the trial stage?[13] Even if these questions could be settled other basic questions still remain, which always revolve around the supposed expertise of the experts, and their right to claim a voice in the sentencing process.

The impetus to adjust the power of the courts to determine sentences has always come from the supposed lack of individuality in the sentencing process. No one really knows how much individualized justice there is in the courts. From the few studies already carried out on sentencing it appears that all courts have some element of individualized justice, the amount varying from area to area, and from court to court. Certain specialist courts such as the appeal court have been studied but it is not possible to generalize from this rather unique case. However, the Court of Appeal has an important influence on lower courts by setting precedents for sentencing practice. As far as the Court of Appeal is concerned it appears, according to David Thomas, to operate on the basis of first making a primary decision to see whether an individualized sentence should be passed or whether the sentence should be on the tariff basis.[14] Decisions to sentence under the individualized method are likely to occur when there is a need to avoid a long period of imprisonment, particularly if this is linked with an expression of faith in the appellant's prospects of rehabilitation by a probation officer or some similar person. Individualized sentences are also likely to occur in cases where the offender has striven to rehabilitate himself but lapsed after a period of success, and finally where the court sees a man in his middle or late thirties clearly heading for a lengthy period of imprisonment and he is given a chance to abandon his criminal career by placing him on probation.[15] Even when these factors are present it does not automatically follow that individualized sentences will be passed; the decision to sentence on the tariff may be considered more important.

Few studies have been made of the way other courts pass sentence, largely because each court is different in its own way. Hogarth's important study of sentencing practice amongst Ontario magistrates suggests that magistrates sentence according to individual penal philosophies, those believing in the rehabilitative ideal using more individualized penal measures than others.[16] As far as England and Wales are concerned, the offence seems to be of overriding importance with some offences precluding the possibility of individualized sentencing altogether. McClintock's study of violent offenders illustrates the point well:

> There was an almost complete absence of any reformative measures. The Courts hardly ever remanded an offender for a psychological or medical report. Probation was rarely imposed and a requirement to undergo medical or psychological treatment was almost unknown. In general one of two sanctions were applied: the fine and imprisonment.[17]

Similarly as far as sexual offences were concerned, Radzinowicz found:

> The preponderance of short-term sentences indicates that the attention of the Court was not directed towards reformative treatment but towards punishment and the possible deterrence of others. Moreover in inflicting punishment the sentence was determined by the gravity of the particular offence. It often appeared that the Courts regarded the mentality of such people as not fundamentally different from that of those who had for instance committed offences against property. They accepted that frequently the offences had been committed deliberately or that the offenders had made no efforts to resist impulses which led to the commission.[18]

Roger Hood in his study of motoring offenders also found that magistrates did not individualize sentences.[19] On the other hand in my own study of drug offenders sentenced at central London courts a high proportion were remanded for reports and a higher proportion were subsequently placed on probation — many with conditions of psychiatric treatment attached to their orders — than for other indictable offences.[20] However, in a follow-up study of sentencing of drug offenders in three South Coast towns the courts appeared to operate much more on a tariff system. Perhaps the offence was of less importance than the local area conditions. The social class composition of the bench and the court area may be important, as Hood for example found differences in sentencing practice where middle class magistrates dealt with working class offenders in relatively small and stable middle class communities.[21]

Given the small number of studies available the only conclusion we can draw is that the use of individualized sentencing seems to be related to the type of offence but even this may vary in different geographical areas. However, if we accept Hogarth's point that sentencing is a very personal matter, it seems that courts routinely process offenders according to their highly personalized value systems. These value systems may or may not be related to individualization or rehabilitation. If they are related to rehabilitation, it does not mean that these magistrates sentence less severely. In fact on the available evidence the reverse appears to be true. Hogarth makes the point that:

> It is interesting to note an apparent relationship between punitive behaviour and 'modern' thinking . . . . In fact concern for justice, a doctrine considered old fashioned and out of date by some appears to have a number of redeeming features . . . . Magistrates with high justice scores appear to impose upon themselves certain restrictions on the degree to which they will interfere in the life and liberty of the subject solely by reason of the fact that an individual has committed an offence. In practical terms a person who has committed a fairly minor offence should consider himself fortunate to come before a magistrate concerned with 'justice' rather than one interested in either his correction through punishment or in being 'modern'.[22]

More specifically, Stanton Wheeler concluded that severity of sanctions appears to be positively related to the degree to which a judge uses a professional humanistic social welfare ideology in making his decisions. Wheeler was surprised by these results but like Hogarth concluded that when a person absorbs a social welfare ideology he begins to regard penal institutions as 'therapeutic', rather than as institutions which are essentially punitive and designed for the community's protection. Wheeler suggests that acceptance of a welfare ideology also leads to a heightened awareness of possible dangers and pathologies which in turn leads to a more sensitive view of delinquency. Inevitably once one begins to see possible dangers and pathologies as being inherent in individual families, institutional settings quickly become regarded as therapeutic.[23] Whether such a view is shared by the offender is of course another matter. The Italian criminologist Garofalo asserted that 'The mere deprivation of liberty, however benign . . . is undeniably punishment', and to tell someone he is being locked up for his own good will in these terms still be regarded as a punishment.

Francis Allen rephrased the point and said that measures which subject individuals to deprivation of liberty contain an inescapable punitive element. This reality is not altered, says Allen, by a motivation to provide therapy or otherwise contribute to the person's well-being or reform.[24] It would be interesting to know how the 1969 Children and Young Persons Act affected the sentencing practice in juvenile courts and whether the children altered their perception of penal institutions when the idealogical approach was changed. Is a care order seen by a juvenile as 'nick', like the old approved school, or is it now regarded as something akin to a therapeutic milieu? Are social workers now seen as a different type of policeman, able to make decisions about the future of children or are they seen as before? If not, how long will it be before we demand that someone should begin to protect the child from the social worker? It is not unrealistic to demand such protection, for all groups with power are potentially abusers of that power, and social workers under the 1969 Act have a good deal more power than most.

To return briefly to the question of sentencing and sentencing panels: it ought not to be forgotten that all disparities about sentencing are disparities within a fairly restricted range. The courts as they are at present constructed have a series of built-in constraints operating at both a formal and an informal level. The Court of Appeal is the most obvious formal constraint with its ability to reduce sentences, but even this operates within the body of legal rules which delineate its power. At a less formal level are the networks of relationships within each court. Disapproval of sentencing practices produces controls, particularly as court members require approval and co-operation from junior officials who routinely process the cases to come before the courts. Most busy magistrates' courts operate a tight schedule and police, probation officers, and other court officials need an element of social cohesion if the court is to operate smoothly. Disapproval of the sentencers means less co-operation. Police will occasionally try to avoid bringing a case before a certain magistrate if his sentencing policy is very far outside the statistical norm.

Other informal norms operate too. Judges and magistrates are expected to be wise and merciful, whilst traditions of the bench influence present incumbents when the myths and gossip about previous magistrates are discussed in 'time out' periods. In short, judges and magistrates are not free agents able to exercise a totally charismatic power when sentencing. They have choices, but they are limited.

Sentencing panels would have the same restraints; they too would not be free agents able to dispense individualized justice according to their own theoretical postures. The difference would be that they would probably widen the range of disparities using the social and psychic health of the defendant as guidelines rather than the offence itself. Whether such an orientation would be acceptable to the offenders is another matter. Magistrates and judges after all have a lengthy tradition of sentencing, and their role as sentencing authorities is now well established: panels would have to demonstrate that they could do it better.

If there has been considerable opposition to introducing sentencing panels, there has been hardly any towards social enquiry reports (SERs), yet SERs are the obvious and open manifestation of the rehabilitative ideal. Their aim is avowedly diagnostic and the recommendations in SERs attempt to make the punishment fit the offender. The whole content of SERs is about the psychic and social conditions of the offender and the sentence of the court is regarded as treatment for those conditions. The constraints under which they operate are mainly legal ones and those imposed by courts, who may decide not to accept the recommendation. Other constraints are imposed by the offenders, who may withhold information or even falsify it, and the final constraints are imposed by the bureaucratization of the probation departments.

The SER is a comparatively recent innovation within the penal system. Section I of the 1907 Probation and Offenders Act legitimized probation orders and required probation officers to have 'regard to the character, antecedents, age, health and mental condition of the person charged'. By 1933 most of the reports presented to court were made by Police Court Missionaries whose aim was to protect offenders, in an evangelical way, from demon judges and demon drink. They were partly successful in this and the results led the Departmental Committee on the Treatment of Young Offenders in 1927 to suggest that probation officers, should, and could, provide the fullest information on the young person. Their recommendations were incorporated in the 1933 Children and Young Persons Acts (Section 35(2)). Later the 1948 Criminal Justice Act extended the range of probation officers' duties 'to enquire in accordance with any directions of the Court into the circumstances or home surroundings of any person with a view to assisting the Court in determining the most suitable method of dealing with the case'. Probation reports (or home surroundings reports as they were called until the Morrison Committee in 1962 recommended the term 'social enquiry report') began therefore as evangelical documents which were later transformed into means of helping the court to pass the appropriate sentence. Questions about how they help the court were not, and still are seldom, discussed, and neither is the type of information that they should contain.[25]

The number of reports have increased rapidly in recent years. For adults over the age of 17 there were 162,380 reports presented to the criminal courts in 1971, compared with 130,676 in 1969 and less than 40,000 in 1950.[26] There were in addition 12,960 psychiatric reports sent to the courts in 1971. These followed a remand in custody for psychiatric investigation. There were a further 1,112 reports where prison medical officers volunteered reports without being requested to do so by the courts and another 564 on the state of health only. The number of medical and psychiatric reports sent to the courts has almost doubled since 1962 when there were 7,755.[27] It is not known how many additional psychiatric and medical reports were sent by psychiatrists where the offender was on bail, nor how many reports were prepared by social workers. These are not recorded in the official figures. If we guess at this figure and say another 2,000 then about 177,000 reports were presented in 1971 for adult offenders alone.

Reports are divided into two main sections. The first section concerns details of the offender, his personality and background, and the second section concerns recommendations for sentence. At this stage the sections can be analysed separately although the distinction is largely artificial as the report writers themselves see both sections as part of the same project. Nevertheless, each section poses its own separate set of problems.

Probation officers have only been provided with some general guidelines as to what should be included in reports. These have doubtless been refined by the officers' own norms and those of the probation departments. The Streatfeild report[28], which was the first official report to concern itself with these issues, was reluctant to spell out a comprehensive list of items to be included because the committee thought that individual cases varied widely and reports ought not to follow a stereotyped pattern. They suggested (numbering mine):

1 Offender's home surroundings and family background.
2 His attitudes to his family and their response to him.
3 His school and work record and spare time activities.
4 His attitude to employment.
5 His attitude to his present offence.
6 His attitude and response to previous forms of treatment following any previous convictions.
7 Detailed histories about relevant physical and mental conditions.
8 An assessment of personality and character

The Committee also thought that a report could cover certain other aspects of the offender's life such as criminal associates, gang membership, etc.[29]

No attempt has been made to simplify this list: the tendency if anything has been to move in the opposite direction. A paper published by the National Association of Probation Officers lists eleven major categories to be considered, and ninety-one sub-categories.[30] Presumably the report writer selects the relevant ones. Psychiatric reports on the other hand have a slightly different flavour, some duplicating the SER, and all expressing an opinion about the offender's medical and emotional health.

In spite of Streatfeild's suggestion that the type of information given to the court should be geared to help the court reach a better decision there is little evidence to support the value of this proposal as a sentencing aid. Social background and offender's attitudes are of little value as predictors of further criminality. Streatfeild also thought that actual experience and results of research (as it develops) should be used to check the relevance of particular facts about offenders as indicators of the likely effect of penal treatment.[31] Research has not as yet produced very much information about the likely effect of penal treatment except to show that the best predictors of ciminality are age, age at first conviction, and the number of previous convictions.[32] Hammond's study shows that these three variables are likely to produce better predictors than sophisticated analyses of social history and psychological conditions. Curiously enough, these factors are rarely mentioned in SERs, preference being given to others which seem to have little or no predictive value. Even where the highly predictive factors are mentioned (e.g. homelessness in offenders with previous convictions) little attempt is made to analyse these in any systematic way.

Moreover the 'diagnostic fallacy' in its attempt to relate 'needs' to penal treatments must inevitably compromise with a retributionist position still built into the penal system. Probation officers have to 'second guess' likely decisions and try to effect a compromise within the limited possibilities that remain open to them. So, for example, a young man aged twenty currently on borstal after-care appearing before the court on an armed robbery charge is not likely to be placed on probation and probation officers know this. Some magistrates have reputations and, say, always send to prison people convicted of certain types of offence, and again most probation officers know this too. Futhermore the range of treatments are limited. For offenders over the age of twenty-one the number of alternatives open for treatment is limited to about seven, three of which are not individualistic at all (i.e. the absolute discharge, conditional discharge and a fine; and although the fine can be made partially individualistic in one sense by the amount and time allowed to pay, this is not individualistic in the primary sense of the word). With such a small number of treatments, individualized sentencing must of necessity be a compromise between the limitless needs of the offender and limited range of treatments.

Social enquiry reports do not of course provide the only information on the offender given to the courts. Police provide information too. In 1955 they were given a clear directive from the judges and now provide their own antecedent history. This usually contains:

A factual statement of the previous convictions, date of birth (if known), education and employment, date of arrest, whether the prisoner has been on bail, and if previously convicted the date of his last discharge from prison if known. It may also contain a short and concise statement as to the prisoner's domestic and family circumstances, his general reputation and associates, and if it is to be said that he associates with bad characters, the officer giving evidence must be able to speak from his own knowledge.[33]

It is interesting to note that police antecedents contain all the information for the best known predictors of future criminality. They also contain another element frequently missing in SERs — namely validity, as police have a duty to verify the facts given to the court. Pre-sentence reports rarely contain verified information. Probation officers and psychiatrists seldom concern themselves with examining statements made outside a selected range of interviews. Data are often presented as if they had been verified or at least as if they presented some form of objective truth. Typically statements appear as if they had been verified, i.e. 'Has had ten jobs since leaving school and is currently unemployed and receiving £10.00 per week social security benefits.' A more accurate statement would be that 'He *says* he has had ten jobs'; without verification he could have had eight or twenty. Hearsay statements are not only acceptable but presented as objectifications as to the truth about what has really happened to the defendant over the past few years. The whole format of the report is 'official' producing a tendency to see the document as a scientific account of the offender's social and psychological history. Unhappily no distinction is made between what has been told to the probation officer and what has been told *and verified.*

Whether any of the information given in pre-sentence reports is reliable is another matter. 'Reliability' means that where more than one person collects the same information they all agree on what that information is. The number of previous convictions is likely to be reliable whilst personality assessment is not. Probation reports tend to include a great deal of personality assessments, and probation officers would justify their inclusions by reference to their 'professionalism'. John Hogarth thinks that: 'if research were to be focused on the reliability of information commonly presented to the courts through the medium of presentence and psychiatric reports a number of profound and terrible truths would be revealed'.[34]

As yet there has been little or no research on reliability of pre-sentence reports but work by Eysenck suggests that psychiatric diagnoses are essentially unreliable, and there is no reason to think that probation officers are able to operate more effectively than their psychiatric counterparts.

If reliability is rarely achieved in SERs there is at least some validity about them, if only because they use information presented by the police and other court officials. Often this information forms the basis of the SER but disguised and presented in a different form. Or as Blumberg puts it, 'to a large extent probation and psychiatric reports reaffirm and re-circulate the same knowledge about the accused originally furnished by police and prosecutor — refurbished and refurnished in the patois and argot of social work and psychiatry'.[35] The police at least validate their information and probation officers make use of this. So do psychiatrists, often reproducing word for word the details of the offender's past history as recorded in the probation report.[36] What is taken to be replication is really a form of plagiarism for when two reports make the same point it is assumed that both have observed the same 'facts'.

Courts may require factual information about the defendant's past history but report writers claim to be providing an additional service. Reports are seen by the reports writers as 'diagnostic tools' where conclusions and assessments are based on expertise, or on a high degree of 'professional perceptivity'.[37] Reports which only contain facts and descriptive material are thought to be incomplete. 'The probation officer must go on to make a professional evaluation so that the court is left with a firm impression of the probation officer's *opinion about the defendant*'.[38] (Emphasis mine.)

Traditionally SERs were sentimental appraisals of the offender's situation concerned with mitigating the harshness and inflexibility of the judiciary. An account of his background, particularly if he came from depressed working class conditions would be likely to explain his conduct even if it did not produce a less severe sentence. It became a short step to translate these explanations into scientific terms so that a 'disturbed background' or a 'broken home' was not simply a vague everyday term but a precise medical diagnosis. Sociological concepts such as 'subculture' are now replacing the traditional psychological ones and these are also being translated into a further set of scientific facts. In spite of the change towards science, in practice the sentimental view still retains some impact; defence counsel are more likely to want copies of pre-sentence reports than prosecuting counsel, and offenders still agree to being interviewed because they think it may help their case. However, the thrust towards professionalism by probation officers has meant they now wish to slough off the evangelical image and replace it with the 'professional-adviser-to-the-court' image. Once this happens they cease to be the offender's spokesman and act as professional advisers to the court. They also claim to have expertise to advise the court on the most appropriate method of dealing with each case. Not all probation officers see it this way; some retain the sentimental version whilst others retain the maternal values strongly associated with juvenile justice and translate these into the adult sphere. Institutional pressures within the probation service, however, tend to supplant the older values with a more up to date 'objective' approach. The professional ideology is buttressed by arguments that objective appraisals are more likely to satisfy the court's and offender's needs than any subjective report on sentimental grounds.

The difficulty confronting probation officers is that they believe themselves to be primarily concerned with personality assessment, when they are more likely to be involved in moral evaluations. Terms like 'immature', 'authority problems', 'sensitive', 'agreeable' and 'quarrelsome' *are* moral evaluations delineating moral character. Regardless then of what they think they are doing, SERs enter the field of morals. Thomas Szasz makes the general point about behaviour assessment, which is applicable as far as SERs are concerned: 'Human behaviour is fundamentally moral behaviour. Attempts to describe and alter such behaviour without at the same time coming to grips with the issue of ethical values are therefore doomed to failure.'[39]

Blumberg sees these moral evaluations as 'character assassinations', although it may be more accurate to see them as thumbnail personality sketches. Assessments based on routine interviews with no claim to validity or reliability can rarely be expected to be able to produce anything more. Mathieson and Walker may call SERs a 'professional evaluation' but we can justifiably ask about the basis of this professional task. First, it is based on a very limited contact. If a person is remanded in custody for probation and psychiatric reports it is doubtful if he receives more than one and a half hours of professional time. In Martin Davies and Andrea Knopf's study on the time spent on SERs they found that probation officers on average spent forty-two minutes interviewing the defendant, with about the same amount of time spent on other family members.[40] No study was made on the time spent by psychiatrists but it is doubtful whether this differs in any significant way. We then have the rather curious position of a person remanded in custody for about two weeks at some social and personal cost and spending an extremely limited time being interviewed. The organizational pressures to produce large quantities of SERs account for much of this limitation, but equally the routine and institutionalized format prescribed by the organization cannot be ignored. Reports are fairly standard — or at least the broad headings and sections are — so that experienced probation officers can operate each interview routinely. Bearing in mind that assessment of character can be a complicated task, it is truly amazing that report writers feel able to reach opinions about people in such a short time.

Second, these evaluations are located firmly in the theoretical framework of psycho-analysis. This means that the interviewing procedure typically concentrates on the offender's version of 'what happened' which is then translated into a psycho-analytic form. Other accounts are taken from family members and the final version is usually a synthesis of conflicting accounts with the report writer's own theoretical perspective superimposed on all other accounts. Even this superimposition must be truncated as must be each person's version. The overall effect is described by Cicourel as being similar to a rumour, as rumours inevitably involve a sharpening and levelling of accounts.[41]

Cicourel's point is that SERs require selection of 'facts', if only to present them in a logical readable form. Interviews with clients do not normally proceed in that logical way and so some form of selection is to be expected.[42] Davies and Knopf note that probation officers spend on average almost as much time on writing and thinking about their reports as doing all the interviews, and certainly more time than on interviewing the defendant. The orderly presentation of so many SERs hides the complexities of interviewing and report writing, and it also hides the selectivity and juxtaposition of the information.

To illustrate this point, Kai Erikson and Daniel Gilberton describe an interview in a mental hospital. The resident psychiatrist is interviewing a young man aged eighteen, referred by the local court, who has been convicted for acts of vandalism. His parents have also complained that they have lost their influence over him and do not understand his behaviour.

> In the course of the interview the conversation touches on many passing moments of the boy's short career. He is asked why he seems to get into trouble so often, and he replies that he cannot think of anything better to do, that he has no close friends other than his delinquent comrades, that his mother is forever trying to keep him at home and that he does not really do anything wrong in any case. He is asked about his childhood and he recalls that he enjoyed immensely the neighbourhood where he lived, that he used to cry from time to time for fear of the dark, that he took pride in his reputation for eating well, that he once had an urge to hit his sister on the head with a hammer, that he enjoyed family picnics in the country, that he wet the bed repeatedly when his family moved away from the home in which he was born. He is asked about his school experiences and he recounts his great fear of the fourth grade teacher, his exploits as a young athlete, the terrible dreams that haunted him for months at a time, the day he took the best marks in the class for spelling, his frequent truancy, the vicious

arguments that used to take place at home, his close friendship with an unremarkable boy called Freddy, and the night he screamed for several hours in fear that some fierce creature meant him harm.

The authors' account illustrates how everything may be relevant but the interview proceeds as a historically selected account of the young man's past. Selectivity must occur both in the interview and at the writing-up stage. The authors show at which points selectivity operates.

the psychiatrist is noting those [events] that seem particularly relevant to the case. It is entirely clear of course that he cannot record everything. He becomes very alert and attentive when the boy talks about his relationship to his mother, yet he relaxes when the boy talks about his childhood friends; he notes the bedwetting and the hammer but not the pleasant memories of the family picnics; he writes about the nightmares and the truancy but not about the high marks for spelling. The case history that emerges from this encounter is a highly selective abstract of the information relayed to the clinician, and the details reserved for the file all serve to make it a little more plausible that the young man is in real psychiatric trouble.[43]

It is of course entirely acceptable — indeed inevitable — that some theoretical perspectives should exist in SERs; the difficulty with the way in which they currently operate is that it is not clear where the theoretical perspectives begin and where they end. Neither is it clear how much the report writer's own ideology becomes superimposed on the organizational demands and the general ideology of the probation service. As the process currently operates, there are endless opportunities for highly personalized truncated accounts to appear in reports.[44] Might it not be that SERs written by different officers would provide entirely different reports?

R.M. Carter was concerned with just this issue.[45] He wanted to know how probation officers arrived at their decisions, how alternatives were selected, and how additional information was gathered to confirm, modify or reject the original decision. More specifically he asked four questions:

1 At the pre-sentence level, what is the order in which probation officers gather information?
2 At what point in the collection of data is a decision made relating to the recommendation?
3 Once a decision has been made, may any additional data received change that decision?
4 Do officers develop a style for collecting information and making

decisions? How consistent is the style from case to case?

The results of this study were startling. In the first place probation officers on average used just over four pieces of information before they arrived at a decision, and once the decision was made additional information rarely resulted in any modification. In other words, gaps created by new information were 'closed' by either translating new data in terms of the existing data or by ignoring them altogether. Carter also found that probation officers developed a specific and unique style, each collecting the data in a highly individualistic way. In other words data collection was not random, but more than this, was highly consistent for each officer even though that consistency might differ from the methods employed by other colleagues. Like the magistrates' decision in Hogarth's study, report writing is a highly personal matter. Whereas Norval Morris accuses the judiciary of allowing their personalities to play an important part in passing sentence, the collection and interpretation of data for individualized sentencing appears to operate in remarkably similar ways. The only real difference is that with SERs we have two areas of personality influence whereas without SERs we only have one. We need now to consider whether this second assessment has any overall effect on sentencing practice. To examine this issue we need now to look at recommendations.

The word 'recommendation' is itself an interesting term, and a fairly new one in the vocabulary of SERs. Early reports did not contain a 'recommendation' but an 'opinion'. The Streatfield report was clear on this matter. 'The probation officer should never give his opinion in a form which suggests that it relates to all the considerations in the court's mind. *It is not a recommendation but an informed opinion* proffered for the assistance of the court on *one* aspect of the question before it.' (Emphasis mine.)[46] The change to the use of the term 'recommendation' is not only against the advice of Streatfeild but implies something stronger, something more comprehensive and something altogether more powerful. To Streatfeild, an opinion meant confining attention to the value of probation whereas a recommendation meant giving an opinion in a form which suggests that it relates to all questions in the court's mind. i.e. the nature of the offence and the public interest. In fact probation officers do recommend, and feel free to recommend over the widest possible range of penal sanctions. Whether they are competent to do so is another matter. Furthermore, social workers and psychiatrists also recommend, although their knowledge of the penal system may be considerably less than the probation officer's.[47]

One of the first authoritative statements on 'recommendations' came from the Streatfeild report; only of course the Committee used the term 'opinions':

108

Although it is not universally recognized that a probation officer may express an opinion in his report on an offender we have no doubt that in many cases he can give a useful opinion. In our view the provision of such opinions should be regarded as an integral part of the probation officer's function.[48]

The Streatfeild Committee also thought that probation officers had contact with other offenders, through after-care, and had acquired some knowledge of the likely effect of other forms of sentences as well as probation. They thought that where the probation officer can express a reliable opinion about other forms of sentence this would help the court, although this would not mean that in nearly every case the probation officers would be able to give a reliable opinion on a number of different sentences, and in any case these opinions would be based on actual and substantial experiences.

The Morrison Committee in 1962 took issue with Streatfeild. They did not think probation officers' contact with offenders from other penal institutions constituted sufficient experience to enable them to make judgments about those institutions or about the effect such institutions could have on subsequent reconvictions. A relationship with an offender from a closed borstal may not for example entitle him to draw conclusions about how a like offender would respond to an open borstal. The Morrison Committee concluded that: 'probation officers are not now equipped by their experience, and research cannot yet equip them to assume a general function of expressing opinions to the court about the likely effect of sentences.' Neither did they share Streatfeild's optimism about the future: 'we do not see scope at present for more than a very gradual development towards the function that the Streatfeild Committee envisaged.'[49] In 1963 a Home Office circular agreed with Morrison. One would have expected the matter to have ended there, but a recent study by Peter Ford demonstrated that probation officers have long since exceeded the limits imposed by Streatfeild, let alone Morrison.[50] Probation officers currently recommend over the whole range of penal services — in Ford's study they covered discharges, imprisonment and one even recommended a deportation order.

Mathieson and Walker think that the probation service has developed its knowledge about the various penal institutions and their effects on offenders as a result of the probation service's involvement in after-care. They think that probation officers are increasingly becoming expert in being able to predict the effects of penal measures on offenders and that experienced probation officers (i.e. those with more than three years' full-time service) should feel free to express an opinion about the most appropriate method of dealing with the case.[51]

Mathieson and Walker's paper is one of the few pieces of work by probation officers on the subject of social enquiry reports and for that reason alone ought to be taken seriously. It is also published by the National Association of Probation Officers, and so presumably has some official backing. It is therefore particularly interesting to note that they do not argue for a *general* right to express an opinion (this word opinion is also less evocative than the usual term of recommendation) but want to limit it to experienced officers. They also add that an expression of opinion puts a considerable onus on probation officers 'to balance the needs of society and the interests of the offender' — which is another way of saying that a purely rehabilitative approach cannot be wholly acceptable.

Until there is an official directive, the probation service will doubtless continue to make recommendations. A leader writer in the 'Justice of the Peace' put it that 'the probation officer's role must always be less than the function of the court, were it not so there would be no point in retaining the court in its sentencing role'.[52] (This question has arisen before when we were discussing sentencing panels, and is a perennial issue in all questions about advising sentencers.)

We have already noted that pre-sentence officials do recommend, and that they recommend throughout the whole range of sentences. In fact they recommend in about 80 per cent of all cases. The link between the content of the report and the recommendation is a straightforward one. Based on Carter's study it seems that pre-sentence officials bring to each case their own theoretical perspectives and individual style and decide on a recommendation based on a limited amount of information. Once the decision is made, additional information is interpreted within that framework.

When analysing the use the courts make of recommendations it is useful to consider the recommendations as falling into two separate categories; those for probation and those not. When those for probation are examined it seems there is a good deal of evidence to suggest that probation officers and the courts are in considerable agreement. The study by Jarvis of sentencing in Cornwall shows that where probation was recommended the Cornwall Quarter Sessions Courts and Appeals Committee made probation orders in 70 per cent of the cases,[53] whilst in America, Carter and Wilkins found that over a two year period in the California Superior Courts there showed 'almost total agreement between a probation officer's recommendation for probation and an actual disposition for probation'.[54] The smallest percentage of agreement was 95.6 per cent, and the highest was 97.3 per cent. These results fit in well with an earlier study where 96 per cent of the cases where probation was recommended actually received probation. However, in Peter Ford's study in Britain the results were lower.

What is not known of course is how many of these cases were certainties for probation before the pre-sentence report was requested. Judges and magistrates tend to select cases which fit into the supposed theoretical position of the probation department — they would for example rarely remand for a probation report a person charged with being drunk and disorderly or even for armed robbery, unless there were special circumstances such as the defendant's age. They would, on the other hand, tend to remand juveniles, and minor sex offenders. There is as yet no way of knowing how many of the defendants placed on probation would have arrived there had there been no probation reports at all.

With non-probation recommendations a slightly different pattern emerges. There is less agreement, but not in the direction one might expect. In Carter and Wilkins's study the range of accepted recommendations was between 79 per cent and 88 per cent — or put another way, about 12 per cent lower than where probation was recommended. Where the recommendations were against probation, courts sometimes made probation orders, and where recommendations were for imprisonment courts sometimes made less severe penalties. In this sense Carter and Wilkins saw probation officers as more punitive than judges.

This is not a new finding. The California Department of Corrections found that judges were more lenient than probation officers about who should be granted probation. Similarly Hood and Taylor found that an increase in the use of SERs did not substantially increase the use of probation in their particular sample of 17-21 year olds. Both studies give considerable support to one of the basic themes in this book that the rehabilitative ideal should not be confused with leniency.

Doubtless, probation officers would justify some of these discrepancies by arguing that their recommendations must be geared to the norms of each individual court. They need 'to find out how the land lies'[55] before making a recommendation, if only to avoid upsetting the court and thereby prejudicing the defendant. To admit this is also to admit the 'second guessing' argument, i.e. that one tailors one's report to agree with the court. How much second guessing occurs is difficult to say, but SERs sometimes change from the time they are presented to a magistrates' court to the time when the defendant appears at the appeal court. The language changes and so does the content. Emerson sees the SER as an expression of the theoretical perspectives of each report writer with the perspectives on a continuum ranging from a 'pitch' to a 'denunciation'.[56] Viewed in this way 'second guessing' becomes a method whereby the report writer manipulates his report to get the court to agree to the recommendation. The language used in reports provides the clue. If there is a 'pitch' then aberrant conduct will be seen as an 'isolated incident' or 'out of character' with an overall pattern of normality. If a denunciation, then background expectancies will be used to show how the defendant was 'building up' to this crime, or the crime is seen as the beginning of a delinquent phase. The same 'facts' can be differently interpreted. For a pitch a person will be described as a 'sensitive young man with a good work record', and for a denunication it will be '*in spite* of being a sensitive young man with a good work record'. Notice that the 'facts' are not the relevant features but the moral evaluations attached to these 'facts'. Closure can reduce the equivocation. Similarly reports can change from one level of court to another, retain the same facts but be interpreted differently. Judges require more commonsense explanations than magistrates, some of whom will accept 'psychological' language. Probation officers know this, but by adopting a second guessing role they also devalue their 'professional evaluation'.

One further aspect of SERs needs examination, and that is the lack of confrontation or challenge about the contents and recommendations of the SER. To understand this we need to examine the probation officer's role within the courts. Mathieson and Walker are clear about the probation officer's role. 'Society requires the criminal to be reformed and the client requires his problems to be solved.' In fact the probation officer's role is more complicated than this, partly because it is not true that society requires the criminal to be reformed, and probably no more true than that the client wants his problems to be solved. A more lenient sentence is most likely uppermost in his mind but on the evidence presented above he ought to choose his pre-sentence official with the same care that he should choose his judge and magistrate. The way in which reports are written often shows that probation officers are uneasy about their role as helper and social worker. Language is sometimes chosen carefully to soften the harsher realities of the recommendation. Peter Ford notes how recommendations illustrate a particular type of organizational demand. Recommendations for probation use the terms 'guidance', 'support' or 'help' and those against probation are couched in terms of 'I cannot help him' or 'no formal support is necessary'. The probation officer must guard against offending the court by appearing too direct and also guard against offending the client in case a probation order is made when the relationship with the defendant has already been damaged.

To understand why there is a lack of confrontation and challenge of SERs we need to examine the denunciation procedures in formalized settings, of which courts and medical tribunals are obvious examples. Within formalized settings there may be formalized roles for differing status groups offering different ideologies but the setting is still a potential source of conflict. Conflict can be reduced by appealing to a wider normative structure, or to a more general ideology such as the search for justice, truth and so on. Conflict can also be reduced by informal gatherings where the court staff ceremoniously give parties, make speeches and routinely praise the work of other members.

In courts, conflict is reduced by these methods, but like other decision making institutions, courts require a smooth running and serene atmosphere. The norms surrounding the court also require a sense of dignity, and restraint, particularly where court officials are concerned. The 'majesty of the law' and the reification of law support a dignified solemn aurora. This sense of quiet efficiency can only be maintained as long as there is a structured and patterned set of relationships.

Overt conflict within a court setting upsets this interdependency, and brings the law into disrepute. A probation officer under severe attack becomes an embarrassment. Courts tend to protect their probation officers, and others too for that matter, for fear of alienating or disrupting the role-sets. In short, formal and informal networks all help to produce a sense of cosiness within an organizational setting.

The defendant, however, is outside this network. Why then does he not question the SER? If represented by counsel he will doubtless be advised not to, for the same reasons as before. If unrepresented he will still rarely attack the probation officer. Most defendants recognize the dangers of this, and rightly view court officials as being 'all in it together'. They also recognize that attacks are likely to be counterproductive. Some defendants appearing for the first time occasionally attack, but they can easily be quietened by reference to some procedural point. As Emerson says, most court officials have a legitimized right to denounce others, and in so doing are guardians of public morality. Counter denunciations stand in stark contrast. Denunciations by officials are phrased in terms which suggest their motives are unselfish and concerned with justice, whilst counter denunciations are seen as selfish and motivated only by an attempt to get a lighter sentence.

Probation officers are, then, protected by the formalized setting in which they operate and also by their claims to be client-orientated professionals. It would not take a detailed cross-examination to show that personality descriptions are not based on a scientific footing and as SERs contain statements that are fragile it is as well to avoid any clash whatsoever. If a counter denunciation appears to be successful then the response from the court will be swift and righteously indignant. They could also be supported by references to the offender's own degraded position, comparing him with the obvious moral superiority of the probation officers: 'How dare you, a convicted thief, suggest that this probation officer, who is here to help you, is not being fair.' If counter denunciations are to be successful then they must be directed at other non-official parties. As Emerson notes in studies of legal commitment of the insane: 'those who resisted their own commitment successfully did so by turning on the private party who bore the brunt of the denunciation and not by challenging the professional legitimacy of the psychiatrist who examined them.'[57]

Social workers, as opposed to probation officers, have less protection. These are still not accepted in the courts, and may even be suspected of having subterranean values. The presence of a court officer from the social services department, who is a full-time court social worker and probably an ex-probation officer anyway, provides some protection. His job anyway is to retranslate social workers' reports — sometimes even by rewriting them — into the court's ideologies, and give an account of these reports in acceptable language. In return for this conflict-reducing role, he will be afforded access to the inner circle of informal networks.

Up to this point I have been trying to draw attention to the way in which SERs as a form of rehabilitation operate within the courts. What passes for rehabilitation appears to be determined by the theoretical perspectives of the report writers, and these are likely to vary with each writer. It seems that a commitment to the rehabilitative ideal may not produce more lenient sentences, and that the use of SERs has introduced their own form of disparities. The question remains: Are SERs worth the trouble? The answer is dependent on one's political and social views, and whether one sees them as being primarily good for justice or in Selznick's terms, helpful in serving the proper ends of man. Research will not assist with that decision. Furthermore, probation orders made without reports were no less successful than where a report was requested. Against SERs, it must be remembered that large numbers of people are remanded in custody or on bail for pre-sentence reports, at some considerable cost, and presumably with social and financial hardship to all parties.

What does seem clear is that organizational demands can never be ignored. Consider the case of pre-trial reports,[58] which have always been justified on the grounds that the defendant will be saved a delay in the sentencing process if he is found guilty because there will be no need for a further remand for reports. As the probation officer's aims are directed at seeing the offence as a symptom of some deeper maladjustment, what happens if the defendant decides to plead not guilty? Suddenly there is no symptom, but because of organizational demands the probation officer must proceed as if there were. We then have the curious position of the social doctor diagnosing a condition without any symptoms and prescribing treatment for a social illness which does not yet exist. The alternative is to assume the defendant is guilty, which means seeing symptoms which are not yet there, and proceed as if they were. The compromise is then complete, the organizational goals demand that offenders be processed before they are officially labelled as offenders.

Fortunately the probation service in Britain has not yet achieved the level of influence of its American counterparts. Blumberg, who cares little for SERs, cites the case of Williams v. New York 1949 to provide a graphic account of the dilemmas that have arisen when SERs are accorded the respect or status of objective truth.

> In the very case in which the U.S. Supreme Court upheld the validity of the presentence probation investigation as meeting the due process requirements of the Constitution the defendant's life was at stake. He had been convicted by a jury of the murder of a 15 year old girl during a burglary. The jury recommended leniency which in a murder case at that time permitted a judge to sentence a defendant to life imprisonment rather than death. But the judge ignored the jury's recommendation and sentenced the defendant to be executed. Among other grounds for his decision the judge cited the negative contents of the presentence investigation report as to the defendant's social history including other crimes he was alleged to have committed. While the Supreme Court was aware that aspects of the presentence investigation violated due process in that hearsay evidence is used, it nevertheless upheld the legal propriety of the presentence procedure. Although the report contained material furnished by the police and others that was not presented in open court on the record and was therefore not available to cross examination or denial by the accused or his counsel the report was adjudged not to violate due process.[59]

In upholding the validity of pre-sentence reports, Blumberg thinks the US Supreme Court believed the probation officer functioned in an autonomous role, acting as an impartial mediator and as an agent of the court. Blumberg thinks this view is mistaken, for probation officers are inevitably tainted by their own organizational demands. He draws attention to the fact that SERs do not have to abide by the rules of evidence, hearsay is accepted but is apparently rarely challenged.

6

Rehabilitation in penal institutions

In 1972 the average daily number of persons in custody was 38,328 comprising 37,348 men and 980 women. [1] The bulk of the people in custody at any one time are adults and it is this group with which we shall be most concerned. Borstals and detention centres can be seen as a separate category, for although they are controlled by the prison department they have different regimes and operate under a slightly different ideology. Moreover, arguments about rehabilitation are mainly directed at the prisons, which are seen as backward when it comes to instituting reformist measures. The extent of this backwardness will be the main subject of this chapter.

Arguments for introducing rehabilitative measures for prisoners come under a number of different headings. One general approach as put forward by the Fabian Society (see chapter 1) views rehabilitation as the only alternative to the 'sterility of the deterrent/retribution approach'. The Young Fabians adopt a less ideologically firm position. They see rehabilitation as *one* alternative, and argue that rehabilitation is a reasonable position to adopt since almost all prisoners eventually leave prison and have to take their place in society again. Rehabilitation would supposedly assist in this process. Another view is that prison is a distressing experience, producing a form of personality disintegration and that rehabilitation is a necessary measure to counter these effects. Finally some think that rehabilitation is necessary because crime is by definition a symptom of maladjustment and to prevent recidivism the causes of this maladjustment must be removed. Whichever position is adopted, the opponents of rehabilitation are usually seen as those 'punitive' groups who support deterrence and retribution. This means that the disputes are mainly about ideological differences.

Few supporters of rehabilitation go so far as to argue that prisons should be abolished altogether. Some do, such as the Radical Alternatives to Prison movement, but they would still retain a type of penal institution probably in the form of a mental hospital or hostel where group therapy and psychotherapy could be provided. Most rehabilitationists accept that some form of closed institution must be provided for offenders, particularly those who are a danger to society. In so doing they implicitly accept a punitive position *but want reform to accompany the punishment.* In line with the definition of reform given in chapter 1, these rehabilitationists are asking for reform by the use of punishment rather than reform as a punishment, i.e. that offenders should be forcibly detained in an institution *and* be provided with reformist measures. To the question who should be reformed, the ideal answer would presumably be, everybody who is sent to prison.. The limitations are usually listed as practical not ideological, and practical in this sense means providing more social workers, psychiatrists, etc. Until there are enough staff, rehabilitationists would want the serious cases to be identified and directed toward the available reformist measures.

What would a rehabilitation programme contain? The most comprehensive account has been given by the American Correctional Association. It is worth quoting in full, if only to show how an ideal programme could operate. Incidentally the ACA say that for convenience they use the word 'prison' as a generic term but they prefer to use 'correctional' rather than 'penal' to describe those institutions.

> The essential element of a well rounded correctional programme for individualized training and treatment in an institution for adult offenders . . . include the following;
> Scientific classification and programme planning on the basis of complete case histories, examinations, tests and studies of the individual prisoners;
> adequate medical services having corrective as well as curative treatment as their aim and making full use of psychiatry;
> psychological services properly related to the problems of education, work assignment, discipline and preparation for parole;
> individual and group therapy and counselling and application of the therapeutic community concept under the direction of psychiatrists, psychologists or other trained therapists and counsellors, casework services reaching families as well as prisoners; employment at tasks comparable in variety, type and pace to the work of the world outside and especially tasks with vocational training value; academic and vocational education in accordance with the

individuals' needs, interests and capabilities; library services designed
to provide wholesome recreation and indirect education;
directed recreation both indoors and outdoors so organized as to
promote good morale and sound mental and physical health; a
religious programme so conducted as to effect the spiritual life of
the individual as well as that of the whole group; discipline that aims
at the development of self control and preparation for free life,
not merely the conformity to institutional rules;
adequate buildings and equipment for the varied programme and
activities of the institutions, and above all adequate and competent
personnel carefully selected, well trained and serving under such
conditions as to promote a high degree of morale and efficiency.[2]

Small wonder that in a later paragraph the ACA thought that many
correctional administrators lacked the funds, personnel, and the
vision and ability to translate the programme into action. This in no way
stopped them from asserting, incorrectly in my view, that all correction
which emphasized punishment works against the protection of
society, and that penologists were agreed that prison was most
effective when it emphasized rehabilitation. They did not produce any
evidence to support these assertions — perhaps because none was
available.

We have met many aspects of the ACA programme before; the
emphasis on 'scientific classification', 'full use of psychiatry', etc., etc.
We have also met the value judgment which pervades many of the other
terms such as 'wholesome recreation', 'development of self control'.
Notice that to operate this programme successfully there would need
to be a form of censorship of reading material if the library services had
to provide 'wholesome recreation and indirect education'.

Are *all* these features essential to the programme or are some more
important than others? If so, which are to be given the most weight?
Does it make any difference if an inmate could not accept one aspect,
say religion, and be, in C. Wright Mills's terms, middle aged, middle
class, small town but secular? The question can be put another way.
Suppose the ACA did not view religion in such a favourable light, but
some inmates happened to be devout Christians or Jews; would they
still be classified as maladjusted until, or unless, they became agnostics
or atheists?

The real issue goes deeper than this. The ACA does not appear to
attribute to prisoners the fundamental right to think differently, or
have different values and beliefs. The penal system sanctions behaviour
which breaks the laws, but many would say, as did the Gladstone
Committee in 1895 that values and beliefs are not anyone else's
concern as long as they are not translated into illegal behaviour. The

ACA programme explicitly accepts the view that treatment officials have the right to involve themselves in these values and beliefs and if their programme was ever fully implemented that claim would be backed by executive power. Training programmes on the other hand merely require compliance, they do not extend to the areas of deeper values and deeper structures, and for this reason are more concerned with obedience to rules.

The extent of rehabilitation in prisons has not yet reached the level of the ideal correctional programme envisaged by the ACA. In fact the level of rehabilitation in prisons is probably very low. Staff members, and particularly prison officers, are usually blamed for this but other factors are also accepted as producing barriers to reform. Institutions are old, often designed in the nineteenth century for different ideological reasons and lack adequate facilities for reformist programmes. The ACA's programmes would be hampered by these physical conditions, but there is more than this. Consider the case of work within prisons, which at first sight appears to be a restricted activity because existing buildings cannot easily be adapted to modern manufacturing processes, and there is often a shortage of space and of investment.[3] The ACA want 'employment at tasks comparable in variety, type and pace to the work of the world outside and especially tasks with a vocational training value' but the ACA fail to consider the theoretical and organizational problems when they call for a new work programme.

Sir Alexander Patterson in the 1930s saw work as capable of providing a training in good habits, a way of providing skills, and a kind of occupational therapy to prevent demoralization. As a supporter of deterrence he thought prisoners should work harder than honest men. The evil of prisons was primarily in the idleness they produced. Since 1961 there have been three reports by the Advisory Committee on the Treatment of Offenders dealing directly with the question of prisoners' work. They gave the following reasons why work in prisons should continue, and then added proposals by which present methods could be improved.

1 Every person should make the best contribution to the community.
2 That suitable work if properly organized is a most valuable part of prisoners' training.
3 That prisoners represent a considerable labour force which ought not to be wasted.

The ACTO reports suggested a massive injection of resources. As a result new workshops are being built,[4] and about £750, 000 was invested in the four years preceding 1969. By 1972-3 sales rose to £10.7 millions. Low calibre work is being replaced by 'worthwhile industrial activity': at Lernes prison for example the first plastic moulding

119

workshop for prison industries was opened in 1972, and at Aylesbury prison electromechanical assembly work was introduced for the first time for firms in the electronic and electrical industries. Prison products are now being marketed under the commercial name Prindus. The plan is to provide most prisons with at least two main industrial activities, thus providing some form of division of labour.

Yet this comparatively modest programme produces massive administrative problems, e.g. rationalizing thirty-six manufacturing industries spread over a hundred or more prison establishments. The theoretical problems arise when prisons are seen as a type of penal factory, differing from other factories only by the presence of a security system. But prisoners are not sent to prison because they have failed to be good workmen. They are sent because they have been officially labelled as needing a custodial sentence. In an interesting study on the effect of organizational demands on prisoners' work, Roy King and Mike Cooper show that prisons rarely emulate an efficient industrial organization.[5] Prisoners are not sent to a specific prison because of their industrial potential but are classified first according to a host of other variables such as age, sex, number of previous convictions and then according to the number of previous periods of imprisonment (star, ordinary extended sentence, etc.). Superimposed on this rudimentary classification are others, one of which is the potential danger to the public if the prisoner escaped. Then there are personal and social factors such as facilities for visitors from family so that prisoners will often be placed in prisons near to their homes. Finally there are organizational demands, the most obvious being the number of vacancies within each prison. Within the prison itself there are other organizational demands, such as the problem of getting the right type of prisoner for key posts, such as in reception or officers' mess, etc., and these are usually filled by the smarter and more alert prisoners. Then 'trouble-makers' must be kept apart, violent offenders must be kept away from sharp tools, and finally there are personality factors operating such as 'psychiatric offenders' (or 'dings') who must be allocated special tasks. Allowances must be made for interruptions for personal visits and for visits from social workers, psychotherapists and families. Although one of the avowed aims of work is to teach good work habits by providing job stability, King and Cooper found that the average length of time spent on each job ranged from 3.6 to 5.9 months depending on the workshops involved. This compared with a range of between thirteen months to thirty months per job *before* sentence. If one thinks of six months as being a reasonable time to learn a skill, then 80 per cent of the prisoners in the tailors' workshop failed to meet this requirement, and they failed due to status changes, punishments, and new receptions and discharges.

It needs emphasizing that these job changes were mainly the result of organizational demands; no outside factory could operate efficiently on that type of labour. It also needs emphasizing that half of the sentenced prisoners are given sentences of six months and only one in five of all adult offenders in prison have to spend more than two years in custody. The HMSO booklet 'People in Prison' sums up the position.

There is about a 400 per cent turnover each year in the labour force of the average prison workshop. This is partly because of the number of offenders serving short sentences and partly because of the transfers that are necessary from one establishment or part of an establishment to another. It is a situation that might face a business with over 100 branches each of which changed its labour force every three months.[6]

There is also the problem of the prisoners themselves. Prisons do not choose their admissions. Some prisoners are apparently not inclined to work, others lack the adaptability to take a fairly routine job whilst a small proportion would probably be regarded by an outside employer as unemployable. With a rare shaft of humour, the HMSO document describes some as being like Mark Twain: they dislike work even when another person does it.

The barriers then to implementing reform are partly organizational. To reduce the barriers an entirely different prison system would be required. The problem of work has been selected for examination because it highlights the organizational demands which could of course be applicable, with some modifications, to other aspects of the ACA programme. However, the theoretical problems are the more important for our purposes, which are present throughout the penal system but highlighted in a powerful way in the prison system. We can begin the discussion by reiterating a simple point, that in the main prisoners would rather be elsewhere than in prison. The staff are the custodians, and the inmates are the group who are controlled, having been labelled as the social failures[7] and who are unwilling participants in institutional life. From this essentially simple statement certain important points automatically follow.

To the rehabilitationist, Rule I of the Prison Rules is the important one: 'The purpose of the training and treatment of convicted offenders shall be to encourage and assist them to lead a good and useful life.' Unfortunately the brutal fact remains that to fulfil this aim it is necessary to keep the inmates in the prison to begin with. The HMSO publication gives two aims, and presents them in a way which, as Keith Bottomley says, is unusually honest and realistic.

The aim [of the prison service] can best be summarised as follows. First it is the task of the service, under the law, to hold those committed to custody, and to provide conditions for their detention which are currently acceptable to society.

Second, in dealing with convicted offenders there is an obligation on the service to do all that may be possible within the currency of the sentence to encourage and assist them to lead a good and useful life.[8]

The order in which these aims are given is significant. The first aim is custody; treatment or training comes second. The difference in terminology is also relevant. With the first aim it is the *task* of the services to provide custody, and for the second aim there is an *obligation* to do all that may be *possible*. What is possible of course depends on what one is trying to do. It is not possible for example to individualize treatment in prisons. Individual treatment, as Sir Lionel Fox said, would mean a specially prepared programme for each inmate, to be adapted to his particular needs in the light of a continuous scientific diagnosis. It simply means that the inmate gets what is most suitable for him in terms of what the prison has to offer.[9] Neither does the term individual treatment provide any clues as to the precise nature or quality of the relationship required to change the character of a particular inmate.[10] It is also clear that to insist on the uniqueness of each inmate will not help to provide a penal policy or help develop a penological theory. The range of possibilities for individual treatment within an institution is therefore small.[11]

In one sense the HMSO document is misleading, for it implies that the two aims of the prison service can exist side by side. If custodial aims are achieved then the second aim can also be introduced. But can they? In one sense yes, provided one is prepared to ignore the conflict inherent in prisons, which takes place at two levels. First amongst the staff and inmates, and second between the staff and treatment personnel. Consider first the conflict between staff and inmates, which sociologists such as Schrag, Clemmer, and Terence and Pauline Morris have documented, although not always from the same perspective.

In Schrag's terms the staff see the prison world as a microcosm of the good v. evil dichotomy.[12] The staff's role is to command and so represent the 'good': the offenders, who have been officially labelled as criminals and are expected to obey the commands, represent the 'evil'. Despite the clear distinction between the groups the organizational demands require constant contact between the opposing moral forces. Modifications may be made whilst face to face contact exists but members reaffirm their original positions when they rejoin their own social groups. However, some prisoners may reject their role as perpetrators of evil and identify more with the staff; this as Schrag suggests is a way of demonstrating a sense of atonement. This group tends to remain a small minority, so that as a general rule it is useful to see two separate social systems each dominated by its own group norms. Conflict is minimized by a common set of expectations which permit the undisturbed continuance of each system.

The importance of Schrag's work is that he emphasizes the role of the prison officer as a custodian and draws attention to the extensive system of rules which overtly assist the officers to maintain order. Rules also produce regimentation. Functionally they demonstrate that punishment still exists with prisons, and they also confirm societal demands that prisons should operate under some form of the less eligibility principle. Rules also preserve the good v. evil dichotomy and in turn reflect the values of the world outside prison.

Other research has attempted to document the nature of this inmate social system without necessarily referring it to the goals of the prison or to the staff. This research is relevant to the main argument for all inmate social systems are capable of frustrating institutional goals. The extent and the strength of these social worlds appear to vary; America probably has the most highly developed, and Scandinavian countries have the least developed system. In Britain, Terence and Pauline Morris found evidence of an inmate social world in Pentonville prison[13] but open prisons and busy local prisons may have a less developed system or at least a different one. The manifestation of the inmate social world appears in the inmate social code. One of the clearest expositions is provided by Clemmer:

> The fundamental principle of the code may be stated thus. Inmates are to refrain from helping prison or government officials in matters of discipline and should never give them information of any kind especially the kind which may work harm to a fellow prisoner. Supplementary to this and following from it is the value of loyalty among prisoners in their dealings with each other. This basic idea constitutes the prisoners' code.[14]

Sykes and Messinger[15] suggest a similar code, which has five major principles:
1 Be loyal to your class — the prisoners.
2 Refrain from arguments with other prisoners.
3 Refrain from exploiting others — but if there is a fight don't back out — i.e. be masculine, which Schrag suggests is a compensation for lack of sexual prowess in a single sex society:
4 Be dignified — learn to do your own 'bird'.
5 In any dispute between prison officers and prisoners, officers are

always in the wrong.

The origins of the code are still open to dispute. Sykes and Messinger and to some extent Schrag using a predominantly functionalist approach emphasize group cohesion brought about by the 'pains of imprisonment'. Sykes[16] adopts a similar position when he argues that, as a population of prisoners moves in the direction of solidarity as demanded by the inmate code, the pains of imprisonment become less severe. The inmate social world provides a cohesive group and a convenient reference point for inmates. Functionally the code also reduces personal aggrandizement and deals with the allocation of scarce resources. It also institutionalizes the value of dignity where the organizational pressures and the numerous prison rules constantly reduce the dignity of the inmate. The net effect is to help the prisoner to endure a painful experience.

Irwin and Cressey adopt an alternative position.[17] Their view, which is based on a form of cultural-transmission theory, is that the inmate social system is imported into the prison by members of criminal subcultures. They note that inmate social systems are specific to prisons — mental hospitals for example have no such system. They also note that 'Prison culture is organised around the values of its most persistent and improvable members.'

The origins of the inmate social system are still a matter for dispute. The origins, however, are less important for our purposes than the existence of the culture. From the available evidence it appears to operate in opposition to the value systems of the staff. Not all prisoners of course give active support to the inmates' code. Terence and Pauline Morris point out that some of the more cherished views of the inmates' code are really ideologized myths.

> Prison contains men who do not see that co-operation with other inmates might be to their advantage; men who are mentally unbalanced and incapable of any rational action, psychopathically greedy and selfish men; and men who are social outcasts in the outside world and retain that status in the inmate community. Behaviour among prisoners, far from representing a consistently cohesive reaction to the demands of the prison, oscillates about an uneasy internal equilibrium . . . . Thus at an ideological level all cons must appear to stick together but at the level of immediate reality, solidarity depends upon the constellation of individual relations.[18]

In a similar view Hood and Sparks suggest that inmates pay lip service to the code's prescriptions; they say such things as 'Never talk to a screw' and 'Never grass on another con' but do not necessarily abide by these rules.[19] However, this group may not be influential in prison as leadership among the inmates centres around those who are the recidivists, have spent more years in prison, have longer sentences and have the larger history of rule infractions. This group also has a high visibility of deviance which functionally reinforces the inmate rules and gives cohesion to the inmate social code.

Irrespective of the code itself and the inmate social system, all inmates are presented with a problem of adjustment when they enter prison. They need to accommodate themselves to other inmates, to the system of formal rules and formal relations, and learn to translate their new environment into something meaningful. This adjustment to prison life, or prisonization as it is usually called, was seen by Terence and Pauline Morris as pathological. They thought it varied according to previous exposure to prison subcultures; to the number and duration of sentences; to the degree of relationships maintained in the outside world; the degree to which the prisoners consciously accepted the dogmas and codes of the inmate culture; and finally according to the nature of the prisoners' relationships within prison.

Clemmer, however, did not see it as pathological but as a necessary process of adjustment by new members to a new situation. He thought that everyone became prisonized to some extent, and that prisonization was a form of adult resocialization in which new attitudes and new ways of behaving are learned. It was also inevitable:

Acceptance of an inferior role, accumulation of facts concerning the organisation of the prison, the developments of new habits of eating, working, sleeping, the adoption of local language, the recognition that nothing is owed to the environment for the supplying of needs and the eventual desire for a good job are aspects of prisonization which are operative for all inmates.[20]

The effect therefore was to disrupt the possibility of adjustment to the outside world, and also make the inmate adopt the characteristics of the penal community in which he lived. Prisonization, like the inmate code, is still open to dispute although mainly about long term effects and whether it is a linear process related to the length of time spent in prison. Stanton Wheeler's U-shaped curve suggests that adaptation to the inmate code and the effect of prisonization are at their peak (or trough) during the middle of the sentence.[21] However, even if prisonization is nothing more than prison-specific and thus of a purely transitory nature it also suggests that a new form of adjustment is necessary where inmates are forced to reinterpret their behaviour and the behaviour of others. This reinterpretation inevitably presents a barrier to the goal of rehabilitation which is our main concern. It may not make the prisoner more criminal on release; its main function is to reduce meaningful contact with the other social groups such as the staff. The prisoners' concerns are essentially about time, the amount left to serve, and relationships with other inmates, all of which are anti-social and anti-administrative as far as rehabilitation is concerned. The amount of penetration and control of this inmate world is bound to be limited. Polsky in his study of juvenile institutions found that the values of the treatment staff never entered the cottage; instead the staff were obliged to fall in with the boys' social system.[22]

Whilst there may be some dispute about the more precise features of prisonization there is a certain plausibility about the concept. It is plausible because people do learn from experience in a particular social setting. The prison is a powerful setting from which to learn, if only because there is no escape from the norms and role-demands of that type of institution. Goffman suggests that most inmates learn to make life as comfortable as possible given the contingencies of the situation. There is also a certain credibility about the inmate social code. The principal norms of the inmate code not only restrict contact between the two social worlds but do so in a way which severely limits understanding of each other's worlds, and this is only to be expected given the requirements of the organization and the attacks on the self so graphically described by Goffman as a feature of all 'total institutions'. Stanton Wheeler is surely right when he says it is too much to expect inmates to enter prison motivated to seek a basically new and different vision of themselves.

Attempts to impose any programme, whether it be training or treatment, must in Lloyd Ohlin's words deal directly with the normative conflict. This means being involved in systematically frustrating behavioural expressions of the criminal values and encouraging behaviour consistent with the value system of the staff world. It is not enough to provide rapport between the two groups and expect changes to follow once a framework has been provided. Many of the new facilities in prisons only provide that framework. Recreational features such as sports, television and free association cannot in this sense be regarded as a training or treatment programme but are humanistic exercises and should be welcomed on those grounds alone. They would only be part of treatment if they contained a constructive attempt to deal with the inmates' personal problems. More likely they are acceptable ways of alleviating boredom.

The conflict between staff and inmates is not the only expression of the good v. evil dichotomy. Conflict also exists between staff, particularly between treatment and custodial staff where treatment officials see themselves as 'good' and custodians as evil. In this second area of conflict the inmates play a relatively minor role, at least until they are released from prison. Then the conflict with inmates reappears.

126

Treatment goals and custodial goals have been closely examined by Mathiesen.[23] He sees the principles of security as belonging to the administrative function in prison; a function which involves everyone to some extent but less so for the treatment specialists. The fundamental principle of this administrative function is to supply a perfect chain of command. Ideally the chain should go from the governor down to the inmates, or from the inmates up to the governor, but either way the chain is an administrative necessity in any autocratic institution. Treatment ideologies do not contradict the notion that there should be a clear-cut chain of command, but see it as going from the treatment expert down. Ideally treatment is also 'individual treatment' which means that the inmate should be treated according to his personal needs. Comparisons with other inmates are seen as odious, or at least irrelevant. Treatment ideologies also insist that punitive measures are less effective than rewards, and whilst the treatment expert agrees that some inmates are dangerous these are seen as very special cases, and not typical of the vast majority of prisoners.

Mathiesen highlights important elements of the conflict, which at one level can be seen as a conflict about power, and about who runs the prison. It is also a conflict which can be translated in terms of life styles; the administrator being seen as an autocrat, the treatment expert being seen as 'flexible' and 'less rigid'. Unless the treatment expert has power he can, of course, enjoy the luxury of being regarded as flexible but when he ceases to be a marginal visitor and begins to acquire some of the responsibilities of the administrator he becomes immersed in administrative demands.

Traditionally conflicts within prison — or at least amongst the prison staff — have been phrased in terms of conflicts between the philosophies of deterrence/retribution and rehabilitation.[24] If prisons were not reforming people then it was assumed that they were punishing people.[25] Punishment was conceived as the only alternative. Prisons were thought to be staffed by punitive people such as prison officers, who were presenting barriers to reform. No one appeared to consider that there was a conflict inherent in the two major aims, and a conflict neatly avoided by the Mountbatten Report which said that prisons should pursue a policy of rehabilitating the criminal *and* prevent escapes from the prison.

These ideological disputes are surface activities reflecting a deeper professional rivalry. The rivalry has been intensified by the introduction of the prison welfare officer who ideologically becomes part of the treatment group. The Mountbatten Report placed a temporary halt to the conflict, for in spite of its claims to serve both aims, the report wanted new administrative machinery which would automatically reduce the treatment experts' role and place it firmly below that of security. Keith Bottomley describes the origins of the change when he says that

> Since the mid 1960's when an accumulation of problems centred around the abolition of capital punishment, prison escapes and long-term sentences of imprisonment precipitated a crisis situation which if nothing else meant that certain realities about the nature of imprisonment could no longer be evaded by the prison administrator and by the public at large.[26]

These 'certain realities' have, as Keith Bottomley says, been distorted or ignored by prison officials, penal reformers and even by many sociologists whose commitment to the need for rehabilitation has led them to focus on the wrong issues. Yet at a very simple level one can see how the conflict arises. Psychotherapists may see aggression as a form of acting out which to a psychiatrist committed to, say, treating an over-inhibited personality could be regarded as a form of psychic progress. To the administrator aggression threatens the custodial role and must be curtailed. Prisons are not, and can never be, places where acting out aggressive behaviour can be accepted.[27] Custodial duties are required to protect other inmates and prevent prison escapes.

The conflict is not of course over, even though it may be dormant at the moment. The rehabilitative ideal is a very persuasive argument and as was noted in chapter I commands considerable support. The conflict is not of course without its casualties, one of which is the prison officer. Paradoxically this group was once seen as the barrier to rehabilitation, but viewed in the way that Mathiesen suggests the prison officer becomes more of a casualty than a hindrance.

The role of the prison officer is complicated. On the one hand he may see himself as representing the good part of Schrag's good v. evil dichotomy, but within the prison he may also represent the 'bad' part. Inmates may see him as bad, and so may treatment personnel. He must do the bidding of both administrators and treatment experts. His social class background may alienate him from direct contact with the governor grades but his ideological position is more akin to that part of the institution. On the other hand he has to do the 'fetching and carrying' of prisoners for the treatment experts and incidentally act as strong-arm man when treatment has misfired. Ideologically he has little in common with treatment, and the treatment methods he would support would perhaps be nearer to conditioning theory than psychotherapy. In the main his opinions on these matters are rarely asked, for his job is primarily to act as a discipline officer.

Prison officers have projected a poor image of themselves, but supporters of rehabilitation have assisted with the projection. Few groups have received more pejorative labels than the prison officer. He has been described as reactionary, and punitive, and as a harsh disciplinarian who joined the prison service in order to continue ordering other men around after he had left his previous authoritarian job as a non-commissioned officer in the armed forces. Sociologists too have contributed to the poor image. A description by T. and P. Morris of the Pentonville officers compares them with the worst prisoners, and unfavourably at that.

> Both officers and prisoners at Pentonville are to a common culture, that of urbanized working class . . . . Like prisoners few of them had or were likely to achieve more than white collar status in the labour market. Their speech was punctuated by the same idioms, they employ the same swear words, they both carry little tins of tobacco and cigarette papers . . . . Conditions in the officers mess were often squalid and dirty . . . . Although the staff frequently complained of the poor food, few were inclined to do anything positive to achieve improvement. It was striking how in the matter of eating habits, some officers were indistinguishable from prisoners. Nor were the uniformed staff concerned much about their own toilet facilities, for while they grumbled until washrooms and w/c's were provided, these were frequently in a filthy state comparing badly with the recesses used by prisoners.[28]

Doubtless all this is true, but whereas explanations of the prisoners' behaviour were given considerable scope and sympathy, few explanations were offered for the prison officer except to see him in a wider cultural network as inheriting traditions of members of the armed forces. These omissions are as informative as any inclusions. For example, a selection of prisoners' essays were included in the appendices; there were no prison officers' essays yet some prison officers co-operated with the research workers throughout the study. Studies on the sociology of prisons have rarely given the officer the same consideration as that given to the inmates, yet a prison is more than the inmates. In other words, books about prisons mostly mean books about prisoners.

Now, the issue is not about whether one supports prison officers or not, nor is it about attempting to transfer the positive halo from treatment officials to the prison officers, but it is about trying to understand how these labels arise. Furthermore, it is unfair to single out 'Pentonville' for attack, since the book did more than most to discuss the prison officers' role, when others have mentioned it only parenthetically. The omission is not accidental but stems from a preoccupation with reformist measures. Rehabilitative theories about crime and punishment have a built-in myopia, which inevitably leads to concentration on one area and neglect of others. Prison officers are neglected by reformist measures, whereas the inmate world has been emphasized. But might not the prison officer have a similar world created by his pains of imprisonment and by the negative values which surround his task? Having been cast as 'punitive', labelling theory would lead us to believe that the prison officer will fulfil the punitive role. The reformative or 'good' role has been taken over by others.

Exclusion from the reformative role has not been one of choice. In the 1960s the Prison Officers' Association began to consider their role as more in line with the reformist position. Nothing has come of this, and it is difficult to know why. The demands were perhaps too great and the required change was too sudden but the claim was made none the less. The 24th Annual Conference of the POA held at Dover in May 1963 unanimously adopted the following resolution:

> This conference, being gravely aware of the dangerous trend in criminal behaviour within society today agrees that the Association should endeavour to define what should be the modern role of the Prison Officer in connection with the rehabilitation of the prisoner. It further agrees that in order to enable the Prison Officer to take his full share in this responsible task he be trained
> a) to assist and advise during the course of the sentence
> b) assist in after care following an inmate's release insofar as this may prove practical.

For the first time in history the Prison Officers' Association was committed not only to a policy of rehabilitation of the prisoner but also to a positive participation towards the end. As their Association put it 'This may be regarded by some as a radical change in the outlook of the POA and its members, but the desire to be more actively concerned has always been present; the opportunity is now taken to express this desire in a more positive form.'

The commitment to a welfare orientated approach may have only been an over-reaction against previous exclusion, and it may also have been an overstatement of their case. As a result of this resolution there were pleas for 'realism',[29] and a plea that change should not take place too quickly. One critic thought it would be relatively easy to 'quicken enthusiasm, raise morale and offer a level of aspiration well above that which was first anticipated' but the effect could be less welcome when the aspirations were unfulfilled. Others suggested that it would be better to concentrate on helping the officer to understand the nature of some of these difficulties which surround his work and teach him to do what he has to do well. Driscoll argues this line and suggests that before rushing into a hasty marriage with differerent techniques it would be better to harness the talent already present and direct this to an aspirational level which can realistically be achieved.[30]

Driscoll may well be right but the issue here is not just about giving support to the POA proposals. The issue is about the sense of exclusion felt by the POA when the prison officer has a basic task within the prison. He after all has probably more contact with inmates than anyone else, and in an interesting study on rehabilitation within prisons Glaser found that about half of successful releases attributed to one or more prison staff their change from criminal interests. Inmates' dislike was reserved for caseworkers and deputy wardens.[31] Clearly then a major part of the officers' task has a strong component of personal relations. Furthermore, the machinery was already there for introducing reformative measures in the work. There were reception boards, staff study groups, wing meetings and house meetings for borstals and detention centres. All that was lacking were sufficient members of trained senior staff and staff training schemes within the prison. Some members of the Prison Officers' Association supported that resolution, although how representative were these views is a different matter:

> Those engaged in rehabilitation should be people who are always there and who thoroughly understand the prisoners; people who understand his background outside and his behaviour inside; people who can talk the same language. In the prison world the person who is best fitted to do all these things is the prison officer. It is he and he only who sees the prisoner every minute of his day, who sees him at work and at his recreation. It is the prison officer who because of this personal and constant contact knows the man better than the Governor, better even that the Welfare Officer and it would thus appear logical that he is the man who should be mainly concerned with rehabilitation.

Three years after the resolution was passed the Prison Officers' Association proposed an alternative career structure to include four grades of officer involved in rehabilitation work.

1. Group officers appointed from the ranks of discipline officers with responsibility for groups of 6-11 men with whom they could hold regular group meetings and to whom they should be easily accessible when information and advice was needed.
2. Rehabilitation officers who could coordinate the work of 6-10 group officers, give information, introduce new ideas and sift the more difficult problems.
3. Welfare officers, experienced successfully as group and rehabilitation officers and with some training similar to that of present

welfare officers. These would see prisoners personally about the most difficult personal problems and act as a link with outside agencies.
4. After care officers operating mostly outside the prison in preventative work with ex-prisoners.[32]

Nothing came of these proposals. They were considered by ACTO which whilst not actually stifling them was not over-enthusiastic. The ACTO reports argued for a teamwork approach where the whole staff would be involved in a rehabilitation programme aimed at reaching all individuals at all levels. Criticism of the POA scheme came from other sources, particularly from members of the probation service such as Jarvis. 'Despite all that is said about the prison officers' new role I think we do have to realize that not all of them are dedicated to doing good, that quite a number being reasonably nice people took the job because it was a safe one and seemed not too demanding.'[33]

Apart from the patronizing tone of this statement the same criticisms could apply to any other occupational group. Probation officers are not all dedicated to doing good, and quite a number may have taken the job because it too was safe and not demanding. Jarvis also quotes prison welfare officers as 'doubting the capacity of the so-called discipline staff to concern themselves very deeply with social work in prison'. They may well be right, but there does seem to be a taint of professional rivalry in these criticisms, leading back to questions of who has the 'positive' halo, and who has the 'negative' one.

Proposals for the alternative career structure have, like the POA resolution, not come to anything. These proposals were for comprehensive involvement by the prison officers in a rehabilitative programme, which may appear ambitious but were to be part of a teamwork approach. The alternative has been a piecemeal programme which grafted an element of rehabilitation on to the existing structure and which separated rehabilitation and custody into two areas. The point is well made by Morrison who adds an additional component, that of manipulation. Morrison thinks: 'It is being recognized that when treatment is separated off from other institutional activities all sorts of possibilities are opened up for inmates to manipulate staff and play off one type against another in ways which can only be non-therapeutic.'[34]

Having failed to implement the proposals of the Prison Officers' Association, and equally having failed to implement a teamwork approach to rehabilitation, a more piecemeal set of proposals has been implemented. These were to introduce prison welfare officers. Morrison's warning has not appeared to be heeded either. The results are in one sense predictable, for the prison officers who see the inmates most of all are excluded and a new sort of expert has arrived in the form

of the prison welfare officer. The effect is to contine to exclude the
prison officers from one of the main goals of the prison — i.e. rehabilitation — but leave him with the other goal which is custody. Results are
predictable in another sense too, for having introduced the prison
welfare officer, and incidentally created a certain element of role
confusion amongst other members of the prison staff such as chaplains
and assistant governors, there is no indication that the prison welfare
officer's post has had much effect on recidivism or even on the allevia-
tion of human problems so often faced by prisoners.

The prison welfare officer's role is part of a wider argument that
prisoners require some form of self-understanding whilst they are in
prison, in order to be able to cope when released. The ideal type of
self-understanding is the therapeutic community. The therapeutic
community has had little impact on the prison system because prisons
are not conducive to a community of people geared to help each other,
each being regarded as equals. In practice of course the therapeutic
community is not a community of equals at all, as someone, usually a
doctor, leads the group. He may be first among equals but he is not
equal when other members of the group are manifestly reduced to
being his patients. A therapeutic community is clearly impracticable in
prisons, as the responsibility for treatment is not restricted to staff
members but shared by all and quite importantly by the inmates
themselves. Ardent supporters of the therapeutic community approach
such as J.M. Wilson recognize that inmate involvement might 'weaken
the element of control usually considered essential in correctional institutions for assured conformity of inmate behaviour — particularly in
those institutions of maximum security capacity'. Indeed it would.
There would be no point in categorizing prisoners as special security
risks if they had a major choice in the extent of participation and their
date of release. Therapeutic communities could only work in open
prisons, and there may well be some doubt about that.

Groupwork is a modified version of the therapeutic community.
There are numerous definitions of groupwork, but it usually seems to
have the same ends as all rehabilitative measures, i.e. to provide support
and increase self-understanding. Groups are not ends in themselves nor
permanent units but are comprised of people who wish to share
experiences and derive mutual support. Groups are run by 'experts'
although prison officers occasionally assist.

The success of group counselling as a means of preventing recidivism
outside the prison is not yet known. Conrad says that in California
'success could not be readily demonstrated in statistical tables' although
those with 'middle base expectancy in long-term group counselling
under one leader seemed to show a more favourable outcome than is
experienced by inmates with a low base expectancy'.[35] In other words

those who were expected to have done better actually did better, but even so, a necessary condition was long term group counselling under one leader. Conrad, however, sees results mainly in organizational terms, such as helping the prison to run more smoothly and transforming 'hard-bitten old guards into paternal and friendly counsellors'. The choice of language is important for it indicates once again how prison officers are viewed in the institution. No one talks of hard-bitten old psychiatrists or hard-bitten old social workers. They still retain the ascribed role of being young, fresh and doing good.

The basic idea of group counselling is that inmates help each other, and this can never be a bad thing, but group counselling like most features of the rehabilitative ideal means that treatment is given to the inmates whether they want it or not, and usually given by the professionals. Group counselling was introduced by a clinical psychologist — Dr Fenton — and is still run mainly by the experts. [36] It is worth repeating that prison officers are largely excluded, except as in a supportive role, and it is hardly surprising that they are dispirited. Having put forward concrete proposals for a new role and having had these rejected, and having been reduced to a status subordinate to the new officials plying their own therapeutic techniques it would not be surprising if they reverted to the traditional view of disinterestedness and disengagement. Perhaps their proposals were never realistic in the first place and social distance and a role configuration based on discipline is what they really wanted.[37] If so, then this has been achieved albeit by a rather tortuous route, and it is equally clear that their lowly status has not been improved by reformists.

The prison welfare officer by comparison has increased his status. He has also highlighted the conflict between Rules I and II of the Prison Rules. From lowly beginnings as minor officials often geographically relegated to distant areas of the prison, with no theoretical expertise and with limited money for discharge grants, the old PWOs had little impact on the institution. On the 1 January 1966 there were 101 prison welfare posts in 57 prisons.[38] On that day the probation service was made responsible for filling welfare posts and six years later there were 360. It is hoped to increase this to 420 during 1973-4 giving a ratio for main grade welfare officers to prisoners of 1:100.[39] The PWO is to be regarded as having a fourfold role within the prison:

(a) As a social caseworker.
(b) As the focal point of social work.
(c) As the normal channel of communication on social problems on the outside.
(d) As the planner of after-care.

This implies that the PWO is to work directly with offenders on their

problems within the prison as well as planning after-care, and to work
directly with other members of the prison staff. He is to be regarded as
a 'member of a team' and the duties that 'might suitably be attempted
in a fully staffed welfare department' are considerable. One duty involves
the training of prison staff, others include visits to prisoners' families,
preparation for home leave (see HOC 18/1965) and membership of
certain selection boards.

But what do they actually do? No one really knows, but it is worth
noting that probation officers were reluctant to become PWOs in the
first place. It is also worth noting that with a present caseload of 120,
and an expected caseload of 100 in 1973-4 plus a variety of administration work the actual time spent acting as a social caseworker must
be small. A principal probation officer writing in 1965 describes an
earlier era before the probation service was responsible for prison
welfare.

> According to [a] Senior Prison Welfare Officer during 1962 in his
> prison the number of convicted and civil prisoners was 4240, the
> number transferred was 3000 and the number discharged was
> 1500 . . . [Using] an arbitrary 40 hour week and allowing for leave
> periods the year probably produces 5708 hours — one welfare
> hour per year per prisoner with an additional hour for each leaver.
> Almost like an annual slice of Xmas Pudding . . . .[40]

With an increase in the number of welfare officers more time will be
available per prisoner but not all that much more. Four hundred welfare
officers for 38,000 inmates is not many when other duties have to be
performed such as giving special attention to discharges, to home leaves
and admissions, helping over problems about visitors, recording progress,
selecting and preparing for after-care, etc. This would still only work out
at about 20 hours per inmate per year, which hardly gives an opportunity for deep casework. In large local prisons where the turnover is
in the region of 30-40 people per day, there are even fewer opportunities
for deep casework, particularly as so many inmates are serving sentences
of six months or less.[41]

The real problem, however, is not the shortage of PWOs; this could
be dealt with by an increase in staff. The real problem is the role conflict
created by the treatment approach in a custodial setting. We are back to
Mathiesen's argument again about the clash between the principles of
prison administration and the principles of treatment. The same point
has been made by Pauline Morris when she says the whole emphasis in
prison is on removing autonomy whereas the rationale of much
probation work is to encourage the client to accept responsibility for
decision making.[42] For whether they like it or not PWOs have to work

135

in institutions which they may see as authoritarian, rigid and inherently punitive but which are aimed at operating a custodial role.

It could be argued that too much attention is given to role strain or role confusion; but consider some basic practical difficulties. What happens if the PWO has a 'good relationship' with an inmate and the inmate says he is planning to escape. The PWO must inform the authorities, so what happens to the relationship? Tempting though it may be to say that probation officers have always dealt with these 'authority' problems as social caseworkers in the courts, they have not had to face them with this type of intensity. Furthermore their involvement with the courts has identified them with the authority system. If the PWO does nothing he is explicitly disassociating himself from the primary aim of the institution. This as R.L. Morrison says is a fatal step involving collusive identification with the inmate against the system, against authorities, and against his perceived bad, repressive, punitive colleagues.[43] The alternative is to 'do something'. Inevitably, doing something involves a redefinition of the PWO's role from a helper to being 'just like the rest, no help to anyone'. The inmate could reasonably say that as 'society put me in prison you the P.W.O's are just like society because you don't help me get out'. The end result must be that PWOs have to modify their treatment role in terms of institutional demands and modify it to the point where it ceases to be treatment as defined in the classical casework literature. By this I mean that treatment traditionally involves client self-determination with freedom to tell all to the caseworker and discuss the basic problems. In a prison it may mean that self-determination exists only within a very restricted operational range and any discussion of inner thoughts must be about acceptable thoughts with 'acceptable' being defined as that which is institutionally appropriate. It also means that PWOs are securely linked to the staff, with all that means to the inmates subculture.

Recidivists are not likely to see the PWO as anything else. The opportunities for manipulation are also clear, for recidivists may pretend to see the PWO as they think he wants to be seen. As Morrison says, the recidivist may or may not identify the PWO directly with the authorities; it depends on how it suits his purposes and manipulation. Either way treatment ceases to be treatment and begins to resemble training. It resembles training because a loss of self-determination and a restricted amount of the inmates' psychic world produces an element of social distance which is central to imposition of external values. The solution as I see it, is for the PWO to stop thinking he is involved in treatment and to recognize that he is part of the training programme.

The PWO does not of course deal only with social work in prisons; his other main function is as a planner of after-care. The background to the PWO's involvement is worth stating if only to illustrate the conceptual approach and the type of models currently used. The Discharged Prisoners' Aid Society was originally responsible for after-care. The Maxwell Committee saw these societies as having a primary function to develop and extend arrangements for after-care as an *essential continuation of the process of rehabilitation.* (Emphasis mine.) The word 'continuation' is important for it marks the beginning of what is often called the continuation model or the through-care model. The Maxwell Committee also thought that

> The central object of after-care is to provide such guidance and moral support as will help the ex-prisoner to cope with his personal and peculiar difficulties and to withstand the spirit of apathy and defeatism in which many are liable to drift back into crime. Efforts to encourage and assist a prisoner to form suitable plans for his future life should usually start in the early days of his sentence.[44]

The Committee wanted plans to be made at the 'early days of the sentence', and they also thought that the immediate material needs of prisoners could be met by state agencies so that 'in future the Aid Societies should shift the emphasis of their interests from aid-on-discharge to *personal after-care*'. In 1963 the ACTO report on the 'Organization of After-Care' echoed these recommendations.

> For after-care to be fully effective, it must be integrated with the work of the penal institutions in which the offender serves his sentence, and must be conceived as a process which starts on the offender's reception into custody, and is developed during his sentence.[45]

'Through-care' meant beginning at the time the prisoner was sentenced. Treatment in the institution and after-care should then be part of the same process. Howard Jones thinks this process must begin as soon as the offender enters the prison and should not finish until the after-care officer ceases his activities with the ex-prisoner.[46]

The argument is a bold one but like most features of the rehabilitative ideal, is defective. We are told that after-care should involve personal after-care and should begin at the day of sentence. There are of course two types of after-care, the statutory and voluntary, but for the present let us concentrate on the voluntary after-care. The impracticability of Howard Jones's argument can be shown directly we examine the figures for prison releases. In 1970 there were about 60,000 men discharged from prisons of which 60 per cent or 36,000 had served sentences of four months or less. (That is assuming they received two-thirds remission on a six month sentence.) Now how are the PWOs going to interview 60,000 men and develop a programme of after-care? Even if the programme was restricted to those serving sentences of three years or more it would still leave about 2,500 released each year. Who is to construct this after-care programme? Presumably the PWOs with the help of the probation service — but they already complain of being overworked, and remember, they only spend forty-two minutes each on interviewing for sentences, so it is unlikely that they will spend more on after-care. The difficulties do not appear to have gone un-noticed as it is interesting to note that the governments have not extended the after-care system. Section 20 of the Criminal Justice Act 1961 provided for compulsory after-care for prisoners serving sentences of four years or more and recidivists and persons under twenty-six serving sentences of six months or more, but these provisions have never been brought into operation; more than that, they were repealed under the 1967 Criminal Justice Act. Presumably it is assumed that these inmates would accept voluntary after-care, or perhaps no after-care was necessary at all?

If the through-care model is impractical as far as the outside probation officer is concerned, it is still more impractical as far as the PWO is concerned. They cannot see that number of prisoners unless there is a massive shift to PWO recruitment. It is already difficult enough to staff a probation service without adding to the vast numbers of voluntary after-care cases. It has already been noted that probation officers have limited contact with parole cases — mean number of contacts per month is 2.2; so how does one add the voluntary cases too?

The impracticality of the model is not the only difficulty, for as we have said earlier, massive recruitment *is* possible. The real difficulty lies in the delusive simplicity of the rehabilitative ideal. In this instance it is the attitude of the prisoners who in the main want little to do with after-care let alone through-care, or at least want little to do with the type of after-care offered by current exponents of rehabilitation. Shapland provides an account of his attempt to introduce this type of after-care to nine recidivists, all of whom had served at least four previous prison sentences.

At the after-care offices the first man turned up on the day of his release and he was drunk. Over the next seven weeks the man and three others made sporadic appearances. The high spot was one evening when all four were present together, one man bringing a workmate with no previous prison experience.

That evening was the only time they functioned as a group in trying to help a member. One was out of work. A group member found

him a job but 'something happened'. He did not turn up for work and
never appeared again. Shapland continues:

> By the end of August (i.e. three months after the group started) the
> group had disintegrated and by the end of the year only one man
> had not returned to prison . . . . *One of the implications of the
> project seems to be that much orthodox voluntary after-care work
> for a short sentence recidivist is as irrelevant to his problems as are
> the few months he spends in prison.*[47] (Emphasis mine.)

Shapland's study was based on a very small sample, but a large
scaled study on voluntary after-care by the Home Office Research Unit
came to similar conclusions. Those prisoners who opted for voluntary
after-care rarely sustained a long term contact. Over half called on
one occasion only, and about 90 per cent had ten interviews or less,
usually spread over a period of about four months. The sample
contained a high proportion of recidivists and as the authors point out
some may have been prevented from calling more often because of
a further period of imprisonment or because they had moved to different parts of the country. Although 'clients' were thought to need help
over a long period there were often long intervals between visits to the
after-care unit.[48]

The author of the HMSO research project hoped that the aims of
the community at large, the aims of the probation officers in the after-
care units and the aims of the client would be at one. The hopes did
not materialize for the caseworker and client held divergent views.
Caseworkers saw the provision of material aid as a minor part of the
casework relationship; the client saw material aid as an end in itself.
One major conclusion from this study was that after-care units seemed
to be functioning as second order welfare agencies, distributing
clothing and money and dealing with employment and accommodation
problems. The after-care units were in effect supplementing the
assistance which clients had from the general social security system.
Fluctuations in attendance were related to the days of the week on
which security grants were paid out. Grants did not always last as long
as they were meant to, so that clients went to the after-care units for
further assistance.[49]

The curious feature of these studies is that anyone should have
expected the results to be otherwise. To see the community, the
probation officers, and the ex-prisoner as at one, all committed to the
general aim of solving the ex-prisoner's problems is surely naive and
goes against all experience of dealing with ex-offenders. Having labelled
a person as a social menace it is too much to expect him to desire a
rearranged version of himself which could be provided by the theoretical

orientations of the treatment experts. To expect prisoners to ask for a rearranged version is a triumph of hope over experience. Prisoners have constantly said that 'with a job and digs I'll be OK' but few treatment experts have been prepared to listen. Yet with a job and some digs the prisoner can begin life afresh, and this also means trying to forget about the prison experience. Furthermore, as Glaser found, the prisoners have a low perception of treatment staff, so it is no wonder that they do not opt for long term voluntary after-care.

Statutory after-care by comparison is numerically less important for adult offenders, being mainly confined to juveniles. It still exists in borstals and detention centres, for prisoners serving extended sentences, and for other offenders released from the special hospitals such as Rampton. Whilst of less importance, numerically speaking, statutory after-care highlights again two basic theoretical difficulties of rehabilitation which are inherent in other forms of enforced therapy, e.g. as in probation. First, rehabilitation accompanies punishment because in statutory after-care the ex-prisoner has to attend the probation office, and rehabilitation accompanies that compulsion. Second, statutory after-care as it is currently operated lacks any specific set of theoretical provisions except as a general argument about the welfare or rehabilitation of the ex-prisoner. In practice, however, two broad strands of thinking appear to operate. One is what Dick Sparks calls the neutralization approach, which means that the ex-prisoner is to be given temporary assistance aimed at compensating for, or neutralizing the effects of, prison. Clothing, money, lodgings, etc., all help to re-establish the ex-prisoner as a 'normal' citizen. Neutralization is aimed at being like a bridge in order to facilitate change from one status to another. The other approach Sparks calls the continuation model, which is altogether different but one which is becoming more widely used. Continuation means extending certain features of institutional life into the outside world, and these features may include organized work, therapy and even control. In extreme cases it may be shelter from the outside world such as a hostel or other protected environments. But the fundamental idea behind this approach is as Sparks says, to carry some features of institutional experience into the outside world.

The neutralization and continuation models are of course ideal types. They are not mutually exclusive nor is one model used for voluntary and another for statutory after-care, although the continuation model is more likely to be used in the statutory field (especially in parole, which is a rather special type of after-care anyway). The evidence from studies on voluntary after-care is that the prisoners favour the neutralization model, but if Sparks is right, the treatment experts appear to favour continuation.

The importance of these models is to illustrate the theoretical difficulties of the treatment experts and in particular their use of the social pathology perspective. Social pathologists see crime as an expression of a personal failure to live up to required standards, but the problem is always defined in terms of the prisoner's failings. Implicit in this approach is a special type of consensus model which always operates in the experts' favour. The widespread desire amongst recidivists to blame others for their own failures is often interpreted as the prisoner's problem without appearing to accept that most ex-prisoners are at the lowest point in the class structure and likely to stay there given the present structure of society. Treatment experts also fail to see recidivism as a reasonable alternative career not related to personal failings but decided on a rational basis as with any other career. Always, the offender is urged to get rehabilitated.

This type of consensus model is operated by experts at the time the offender is released from the institutions. The model used within prison permits more institutionalized disagreements as would be expected within a regime where a large group, i.e. the inmates, are unwilling parties. With statutory after-care − as indeed with probation generally − conflicts are minimized by the treatment staff who see 'the problem' in terms of the prisoner's personality. The after-care authorities are then placed in the rather curious position of trying to enforce their own consensus model and continuing a treatment programme based on an earlier model which had more inherent conflict.

In order to operate a rehabilitative model throughout the sentence and continuing through the after-care stage, two features of the present system need to be changed. The first is to reduce the 'concomitant regimentation of the prisoners' daily life' or put another way, to provide some autonomy for prisoners in the decision making process. Second, the system would need to provide a greater emphasis on personal relations with a corresponding change in attitudes to authority. Both are key issues in any rehabilitation programme. The difficulty is that the custodial aim reduces the impact of the first one, whilst the treatment experts reduce the second. First, there are limits to the amount of autonomy inmates can be given in a maximum security setting, for the very nature of that setting means that inmates have to be given constant supervision. Furthermore improvement in the quality of personal relationships means improvement at all levels, so this will mean including the prison officers. More than that it means including the prison officers on after-care too. The continuation model means exactly what it says if it is to be applied properly, i.e. relationships are to be continuous and not divorced from those who see most of the prisoners.

Perhaps too much is being made of the point. All prisoners do not view prison in these terms at all, preferring to see it as a form of retribution where they pay for their offences, and would not expect it to be otherwise. Having paid the penalty, after-care seems to them nothing more than a way of apologizing for having inflicted pain in the first place. Perhaps prisoners view it simply in those terms; there is, after all, considerable evidence to suggest that a 'tough minded' attitude is associated with working class values and prisoners are for the large part working class. On the other hand, perhaps the only conflict seen in prisons is the difference between what is supposed to happen and what does happen. Thomas Mathiesen calls this 'censoriousness'[50] which he defines as criticisms of those in power for not following in their behaviour, principles that are established as correct within the social system in question. Like Goffman's mental patients the prisoner has been made into a prisoner, told he will be rehabilitated but never actually receives any rehabilitation. Perhaps this is the conflict, that the prisoner feels cheated and let down.

What does seem clear is that prisoners are not enamoured with the after-care system preferring to define it as a supplier of material needs rather than a way of providing insights. The soul-doctors are not to their liking. If any message is clear it is that prisoners ought to be listened to more often, and listening to them does not mean interpreting what they say. Prisoners say, 'with a job and digs I'll be OK', they do not not say 'with a job, with digs and some insights I'll be OK'. The prisoners' aims are less grandiose, but on humanitarian grounds rather than treatment grounds they ought to be given some credibility. Aftercare could begin, and end at that point, unless or until prisoners ask for that 'something else' which they do not appear to have done so as yet.

7

A personal overview

The central concern of this book has been with rehabilitation. The discussion has operated at two levels, first to examine rehabilitation as a concept, and second to show that the implementation of that concept has led to some strange and curious results. I have tried to show that it is, if I might use Professor Flew's term, a shambles. It means, as I understand it, that offenders require and need understanding, and as a result of this understanding they will receive insights which will substantially alter their attitudes. This will prevent them from committing further offences. The methods used are mainly psycho-therapeutic so that a relationship with a therapist provides the basis for treatment. All offenders are, by definition, thought to need treatment, and since offenders have different personalities, treatment must be individualized.

The conceptual shambles begins when we considered the social pathology perspective and the individualization of sentencing. In chapter 2 I tried to show that social pathology was inappropriate to crime and deviancy and in the chapters concerned with individualized treatment I tried to show that there were numerous conceptual and theoretical difficulties which introduced some dilemmas, particularly for the experts. The net effect has been to produce in Matza's terms 'a system of rampant discretions'. What then needs to be changed? Or to put the question another way, is it possible to reduce the rampant discretions in a way which is both practical and feasible? In one sense yes, but the history of penal system shows that change must of necessity be comparatively slow, and must at the same time preserve a system of balance between what Weber called 'vending machine' justice and individual discretions. The basis of my argument is that discretions are more in the hands of the experts than with the judiciary. The balance has shifted, and shifted in a way which has not always been in accordance with the offender's interests, nor in accordance with basic notions of fairness.

Now it is both understandable and acceptable that people involved in making important decisions should have their advisers. It is equally understandable that some discretions should be permitted in the decision making process and no doubt the debate has, and will always be, about the amount of discretion available. Where the rules are clearly formulated, and where sentences are determined by those rules, the system becomes inflexible. Conversely, where there are rules which permit discretion, the system produces powerful groups able to stamp their authority on that discretionary area. In the penal system as it currently operates there are wide discretionary powers. Davis made the point about discretion in a way which must be considered a definitive statement on this issue.

> Where law ends, discretion begins, and the exercise of discretion may mean either beneficence or tyranny, either justice or injustice, either reasonableness or arbitrariness.[1]

Discretionary powers exist at the sentencing stage and particularly at the point where mitigating circumstances can be considered. They also exist at key points within the sentence and would assume greater emphasis if sentences were indeterminate. As it is, discretionary powers are also present in the type of treatment or training that the offender now receives. In current practice, it is possible to identify three major areas of discretion; the pre-sentence stage, the allocation stage and the release stage. It is important to remember that within these key areas they are *all* dominated by the rehabilitative ideal. It is also important to note that there is an absence of debate about these areas; non-rehabilitationists for example have little say in the preparation of social enquiry reports and yet social enquiry reports are essentially a key area in discretion. Offenders may not know, but they should learn to choose their report writer with great care since the chances of being placed on probation or going to prison have a great deal to do with that report writer.

In order to operate the treatment model successfully there need to be wide discretionary powers. Discretion is the essence of rehabilitation. In the past where more discretionary powers have been given, they have been used by the experts. Consequently any increase in such discretion has not led to a corresponding increase in discussion nor has there been any attempt to hammer out basic principles. More discretion has simply led to demands for even more discretion. The net effect has been a 'degeneration into more speculation, uninformed either by any clear purpose or by information relevant to possible secondary aims'.

Discretionary powers may be essential to rehabilitation, but if used widely they are antithetical to notions of fairness. Rehabilitation deals with personality facets which by their very nature are oblique and not always open to objective assessments. In order to reduce the relative power of the experts a closer scrutiny could be made of the ways in which they operate. Davis believes that *openness* is a most important instrument for reducing arbitrary powers, for openness 'is a natural ally in the fight against injustice'. [2] Without being too optimistic about Davis's suggestion he has made an important point, for throughout this book certain key areas abound with secret documentation and unqualified individual intuitions. Openness can obviously mean many different things and so there is a need to be specific about which areas should be opened.

One way of introducing openness would be at the point where the SER was presented to the court. A more rigorous cross-examination could be made of its contents. Medical and psychiatric reports could be more open too. When this has been suggested in the past the opposing arguments have been made on the grounds that openness would reduce the quality and content of information that would be given. Probation officers and psychiatrists would say less if they knew they were to be challenged.[3] Furthermore, the offender would be adversely affected if he knew that, say, he had been diagnosed as schizophrenic. All this may be true but if information cannot stand up to challenge and cross-examination is it really the sort of information that helps the court and would the offender really be affected if he knew he was schizophrenic? Probably not, and anyway he would have to find out sometime, so why not then. The alternative is to continue with the present system where the offender sees pieces of paper passed from one court official to another, and knows that they are about him but is unable to see them. Openness in this context is probably more desirable than secrecy.

Although the operation of any penal system is about balance, there are various types of balances. There is one between discretion and a rigid legal framework which results in the balance between openness and secrecy. There is also another balance, and that is between openness and what is legitimately private, and this balance is no less difficult to strike. Should the background of the offender be a matter between him and the court or is this a matter for everybody? Should the public know why an offender has been released on parole or is that a matter for the favoured few or only a matter between the offender and the institution? Having once established a more open system, the debate must still go on but hopefully it would shift away from discussing openness to one where the discussion was about the rights of the

145

offender, or put another way, where one set of rights conflicts with another sets of rights. No clear-cut answers are likely to be made but equally there are less likely to be answers if there is no debate at all.

The question of openness is not of course restricted to SERs but could include other areas too. Indeterminate sentences (or semi-indeterminate to be more accurate as far as Britain is concerned) have found support amongst rehabilitationists but are areas which permit arbitrary power. Again, as far as juvenile justice is concerned, the care order is semi-indeterminate and in a recent visit to a community home (previously an approved school) the major complaint amongst the inmates was that they did not know their date of release. Immense power is then given to treatment officials who may justify their position on the grounds that they are acting for the inmates' benefit and welfare — but do the inmates see it this way? C.S. Lewis distinguished between the helpers and the others when he said of a young woman that 'she lives for others, you can tell the others by the haunted look on their faces'.[4] Adult prisoners may not have that haunted look but Herschel Prins is right to draw our attention to the possibilities of coercion, manipulation and intolerance surrounding much of the rehabilitative ideal.[5] This is not to devalue the desire to do good, or like Elizabeth Fry, to be useful, but doing good and having power can be a devastating mixture. Retributive controls at least counteract this type of arbitrary power.

But the really key question still remains. Should the penal system be permitted to operate a system of enforced therapy and should people be sentenced to receive help? At a very personal level my answer would be a tentative no. In saying that, I recognize that the implications of such an answer would be profound, but it must be emphasized that I am not saying that offenders should be deprived of social work help or even of therapy. Such services ought to be available to them as they are to everyone else, but this is not the same as saying that help and therapy should be built into the sentence, or even made a condition of that sentence. This would effectively mean that treatment would operate on the same basis as voluntary after-care, and the probation service would be available to anyone who wanted to use it.

To operate successfully, probation officers would of course have to compete with other groups offering different ideologies all concerned with helping the ex-prisoner. They could also be available to speak for the offender in court. Some offenders do ask for someone to speak for them and probation officers are admirably suited for this role. Not all offenders are articulate or self assured in courts, and there are first offenders who do not know procedure well enough to give an adequate account of themselves. Such an account would differ from a legal defence but would be additional to mitigating circumstance. The difference between the present and intended method would be that probation officers should have no part of the current method of providing thumbnail character sketches so prevalent in social enquiry reports. Probation as a sentence aimed at rehabilitating offenders would disappear to be replaced more as a supervisory sentence rather than one aimed at helping with the offender's personality problems. The psychiatrist's role would also be reduced, having no expert part to play in the sentencing or allocation procedure. He too would operate in the same way as probation officers, i.e. treating people who want that sort of help. Coercive help would no longer operate. In penal institutions, training programmes would replace treatment programmes with an emphasis on external controls, and where statutory after-care exists, it would be as a continuation of training. In opting for a training programme rather than treatment, I am assuming that the state will always reserve the right to impose external controls on an offender but training programmes at least do not have the disadvantages of treatment, neither do they give state officials the legitimate right to inquire into the personal lives of labelled deviants.

Why then, only a tentative answer rather than a positive full-blooded one? The reason is simple, that before decisions are made in the penal system there must be full and frank discussion. There will always be crime and will always be a need to shut some offenders away from society. The issues raised by the statement are perennial ones; who decides, who is to be punished, for how long, and for what reasons, are not questions that can be decided easily. Consequently I keep asking for a debate and above all a debate where labels such as punitive, reactionary, weak and permissive are not the controlling forces. In this book I have tried to pose some of the questions; hopefully others will continue the discussion.

NOTES

Chapter 1   Rehabilitation – an overview

1   HMSO 'Report of the Departmental Committee on Prisons', 1895, Cmd 7703.
2   See McClean, J.D. and Wood, J.C., 'Criminal Justice and the Treatment of Offenders', Sweet & Maxwell, 1969, ch. 5 for a discussion on some basic legal requirements of juvenile justice.
3   Ibid. for an account of 'mens rea'.
4   Allen, Francis A., Criminal Justice, Legal Values, and the Rehabilitative Ideal, 'Journal of Criminal Law, Criminology and Police Science', 1959, vol. 50, pp. 226-32.
5   Anttila, I., Conservative & radical criminal policy – Nordic countries, 'Scandinavian Studies, in Criminology', 1971, vol. 3, p. 10.
6   HMSO 'Royal Commission on the Penal System', 1967, vols 1-4. Most of the quotes are taken from vol. 4.
7   Ibid., vol. 2.
8   Allen, Francis A., op. cit.
9   Hood, R.G., Homeless Borstal Boys, 'Occasional Papers in Social Administration no. 18', Bell, 1966.
10 See particularly Benn, S.I. and Peters, R.S., 'Social Principles and the Democratic State', Allen & Unwin, 1959, ch. 8, for a first class discussion on punishment.
11 Both quotes from HMSO 'Royal Commission on the Penal System', 1967, vol. 4, p. 77.
12 Ibid., vol. 4, p. 35.
13 Ibid., vol. 2, p. 93.
14 American Correctional Association, Development of Modern Correctional Concepts and Standards, in Carter, R.M., Glaser, D. and Wilkins, L.T. (eds), 'Correctional Institutions', Lippincott, 1972, p. 21.
15 There are numerous texts on punishment but see particularly Hart, H.L., 'Punishment and Responsibility', Oxford University Press, 1968.
16 American Correctional Association, op. cit., p. 25.

17   Cloward, R.A., Social Control in the Prison, in SSRC 'Studies in the
      Social Organisation of the Prison', 1960.
18   Flew, A., 'Crime or Disease', Macmillan, 1973.
19   Glueck, S. 'Law and Psychiatry', Johns Hopkins Press, 1962, p. 148.
20   Jackson, George, 'Soledad Brother', Jonathan Cape/Penguin, 1971. See
      introduction by Jean Genet.
21   For a discussion on these three approaches see Schur, Edwin. M., 'Radical
      Non-Intervention', Prentice-Hall, 1973.
22   Chapman, D., 'Sociology and the Stereotype of the Criminal', Tavistock,
      1968, p. 4.
23   Lemert, Edwin M., 'Social Action and Legal Change', Aldine, 1970.
24   Berger, P. and Luckmann, T., 'The Social Construction of Reality', Allen
      Lane, 1967, p. 104.
25   Mill, J.S., 'On Liberty', Blackwell, 1946.
26   Sparks, R.F., The Depraved are not just Deprived, 'New Society', 24
      July 1969.
27   Matza, D., 'Delinquency and Drift', Wiley, 1964.

Chapter 2   Rehabilitation, crime and law

1   HMSO, 'Royal Commission on the Penal System', 1967, vol. 1,
      p. 93.
2   Jeffrey, C.R., Positivism and the Classical School, in Mannheim H. (ed.),
      'Pioneers in Criminology', Stevens, 1960.
3   Also to be included would be the availability of witnesses, and availability
      in this sense also means whether witnesses would be prepared to assist the
      police in any prosecution and not just whether anyone saw the crime being
      committed.
4   See particularly Bottomley, A. Keith, 'Decisions in the Penal Process',
      Martin Robertson, 1973, chapters 1 and 2 for a discussion on the proble-
      matic nature of the criminal statistics as they apply to the penal system.
5   When Edwin Lemert suggested to Sutherland that his study ought to be
      called White Collar Criminals, he captured the essence of this dilemma.
      See Lemert, E.M., 'Human Deviance, Social Problems and Social Control',
      Prentice-Hall, 1967, p. 14.
6   Rock, Paul, 'Deviant Behaviour', Hutchinson, 1973, p. 132.
7   Smith, John, Guilty without Intent, 'New Society', 14 April 1969.
8   Ibid.
9   See Bean, Philip, 'The Social Control of Drugs', Martin Robertson, 1974,
      for a discussion of strict liability offences in relation to the Dangerous
      Drugs Acts.
10   Chambliss, W., The Law of Vagrancy, in Chambliss, W. (ed.) 'Crime and
      the Legal Process', McGraw-Hill, 1969.
11   Hadden, T. and McClintock, F., 'Social and Legal Definitions of Criminal
      Violence'. Fourth National Conference on Research and Teaching in
      Criminology, Institute of Criminology, Cambridge, mimeo, p. 5, 1970.
12   Durkheim attempted a classification of law. He said there were two types;
      one consisted essentially of imposing suffering, or at least inflicting a loss
      on the agent. This type of law 'makes demands on the sufferer's fortune,
      on his honour, on his life or on his liberty and deprives him of something
      he enjoys'. Durkheim called this type of law repressive. Civil law or
      restitutive law did not imply suffering but was concerned with returning
      things to what they were. See Lukes, S., 'Emile Durkheim: His Life and

Work', Allen Lane, 1973 for a full discussion on Durkheim's notion of law.
13 Durkheim, E., 'The Division of Labour in Society', Free Press, 1964, p. 73.
14 Ibid., p. 81.
15 Ibid., p. 81.
16 Ibid., p. 77.
17 Duster, Troy, 'The Legislation of Morality', Free Press, 1972.
18 Quoted by Lukes, S., op. cit., p. 163.
19 Both quotes from Erikson, Kai, Notes on the Sociology of Deviance, in Becker, H.S., 'The Other Side', Free Press, 1964, p. 15.
20 Rock, Paul, op. cit., p. 157.
21 Parsons, T. and Smelser, N., 'Economy and Society', Free Press, 1956. Also Parsons, T., 'The Social System', Free Press, 1951.
22 Bredemeur, H., Law and Social Structure, in Aubert, V. (ed.), 'Sociology of Law', Penguin, 1969.
23 White, R., Lawyers and the Enforcement of Rights, in Morris, Pauline, et al., 'Social Needs and Legal Action', Martin Robertson, 1973, p. 15.
24 Dicey, A., Law and Public Opinion, in Aubert, V., op. cit., p.73.
25 White, R., op. cit., p. 16.
26 Ibid. Also see ibid. for a discussion on the merits of the different models.
27 Rock, Paul, op. cit., p. 128.
28 Kutchinsky, Berl, The Legal Consciousness, in Podgorecki, A. et al. (eds), 'Knowledge and Opinion about Law', Martin Robertson, 1973, p. 103.
29 Van Houtte, J. and Vinke, P., Attitudes Governing the Acceptance of Legislation in Various Social Groups, in Podgorecki, A., op. cit., p. 21.
30 Ibid., p. 39.
31 See particularly Zeno, 'Life', Macmillan, 1968, for an intriguing discussion about prisoners' political and social values.
32 Gusfield, Joseph, Moral Passage, in Bersani, C. (ed.) 'Crime and Delinquency', Macmillan, 1970.
33 These quotes are taken from 'Knowledge and Opinion about Law', op. cit., p. 15 and p. 70.
34 The right to be different is the theme of an excellent study by Kittrie, Nicholas N., 'The Right to be Different', Johns Hopkins Press, 1971.
35 Weber, Max, 'Law in Society', Harvard University Press, 1954, p. 303. For a survey on Weber's ideas on law see Schur, Edwin M, 'Law and Society', Random House, 1968, pp. 108-9 and Gurvitch, G., 'Sociology of Law', Routledge & Kegan Paul, 1973.
36 Weber, op. cit., p. 354.
37 Ibid.
38 See Schur, Edwin M., op. cit., for a discussion on the legal realists.
39 Legal realists would argue that juries make law too, if only by uncertain decisions, i.e. by refusing to convict they produce legal changes such as when they refused to convict on manslaughter charges involving driving offences and a new offence of death by dangerous driving was created.
40 BBC, Dimbleby lecture, 1974.
41 Walker, Nigel, 'Crime and Punishment in Britain', Edinburgh University Press, 1968, p. 18.
42 See Weinberg, M. and Rubington, E. (eds), 'The Solution of Social Problems', Oxford University Press, 1973, p. 20 for a useful discussion on social pathology and its relationship to social problems.
43 Rex, J., 'Key Problems of Sociological Theory', Routledge & Kegan Paul, 1961.
44 Mills, C. Wright, The Professional Ideology of Social Pathologists, 'American Journal of Sociology', 1943, vol. 49, p. 169.

45   Quoted in ibid., p. 168.

Chapter 3   The experts

1   See particularly Taylor, I., Walton, P. and Young, J., 'The New Criminology',
        Routledge & Kegan Paul, 1973, pp. 3-11 for a discussion on classical and
        neo-classical schools as they affect traditional criminology.
2   Ibid., p. 8.
3   Jeffrey, C.R., discusses positivism and its emphasis on determinism in
        Mannheim, H. (ed.) 'Pioneers in Criminology', Stevens, 1960.
4   Cohen, S., Criminology and the Sociology of Deviance in Britain, in Rock,
        Paul and McIntosh, Mary (eds), 'Deviance and Social Control', Tavistock,
        1974.
5   Taylor, I., Walton, P. and Young, J., op. cit. pp. 3-4.
6   Freud was a product of his time in another sense too, for he was able to
        demonstrate that he was part of the expanding world of medicine as well
        as fitting into the masculine orientated world with theories constantly
        exalting the male role.
7   Briar, S. and Miller, H., 'Problems and Issues in Social Casework',
        Columbia University Press, 1971, p. 10.
8   Quoted in ibid., p. 10.
9   The nineteenth century philanthropists such as Octavia Hill had always
        emphasized the mental component of poverty. The British social worker of
        the 1920s may have been more influenced by the Americans than by
        Octavia Hill but the psychiatric social worker was nevertheless in line with
        psychiatric traditions long before it was acquired from the USA.
10   Wootton, Barbara, 'Social Science and Social Pathology', Allen & Unwin,
        1960, p. 270.
11   Flew, Anthony, 'Crime or Disease', Macmillan, 1973, p. 19.
12   See Wootton, Barbara, The Law, the Doctor and the Deviant, 'British
        Medical Journal', 21 July 1963, for an alternative discussion on these
        three roles.
13   Quoted in ibid., p. 197.
14   Blumberg, A.S., 'Criminal Justice', Quadrangle Books, 1967.
15   Szasz, T., Psychiatric Expert Testimony, 'Psychiatry', 1957, vol. 20, no. 3,
        p. 313.
16   Henry Steadman views the psychiatrist's role in the American court as an
        error forced upon the courts by psychiatric incompetence in the last
        century. Psychiatrists originally entered the courts because of the public's
        concern to check their absolute power. Apparently, in the 1870s a number
        of people in America had been 'railroaded' into mental hospitals and only
        after some aggressive lobbying did Illinois pass the first American commit-
        ment law. Steadman says the psychiatrist did not become involved in the
        courtroom because he was an expert witness but as a result of a demand for
        safeguards. Steadman, H., The Psychiatrist as a Conservative Agent of Social
        Control, 'Social Problems', 1972, vol. 20, no. 2, p. 269.
17   Steadman also suggests that psychiatrists prefer to play safe and argue for
        hospital admissions because of a fear of repercussions if offenders commit
        further offences (ibid.). See also McGarry, A., The Fate of Psychotic
        Offenders Returned to Trial, 'American Journal of Psychiatry', 1971, vol.
        127, p. 10.
18   See Walker, N. and McCabe, S., 'Crime and Insanity in England', Edinburgh
        University Press, 1973, vol. 2, p. 273, for a further discussion on

these figures.

19 Offenders are usually encouraged to be frank during an interview because it is suggested frankness will help the offender in the long run. The crucial question is, will it?

20 Wootton, Barbara, The Law, the Doctor and the Deviant, op. cit.

21 Ibid., p. 200. See also Szasz, T., 'Law, Liberty and Psychiatry', Routledge & Kegan Paul, 1974.

22 This is particularly true of the Home Office Probation courses where about half the lecturers are psychiatrists.

23 See particularly Rosenberg, A. and McGarry, L., Competency for Trial, the Making of an Expert, 'American Journal of Psychiatry', 1972, vol. 128, p. 85.

24 Lerman, Paul, 'Delinquency and Social Policy', Praeger, 1970, p. 5.

25 Allen, Francis A., Criminal Justice, Legal Values and the Rehabilitative Ideal, 'Journal of Criminal Law, Criminology and Police Science', 1959, vol. 50, p. 299.

26 Weschsler, H., Law, Morals and Psychiatry, 'Columbia Law School News', 2 April 1959, vol. 13, p. 4.

27 See Prins, Herschel, Non Custodial Measures and the Criminal Justice Act, 1972, 'Prison Service Journal', January 1974, for a discussion on the measures.

28 Jarvis, F., 'Manual of Probation', Butterworth, 1969, p. 40. This book also gives a summary of the background and duties of the Probation Officers.

29 Szasz, T., Moral Conflict and Psychiatry, 'Yale Review', Summer 1960, vol. 49.

30 HMSO 'Preliminary Report of the Probation Research Project', 1966.

31 Eshelby, S.R., The Probation Officer as a Caseworker, quoted in Younghusband, E. (ed.), 'New Developments in Casework', Allen & Unwin, 1966, p. 11.

32 Monger, Mark, 'Casework in After-Care', Butterworth, 1967, p. 47.

33 Blumberg, A.S., op. cit., p. 156.

34 Weber, Max, 'The Theory of Social and Economic Organization', Free Press, 1964, p. 340.

35 Hood, R.G. and Sparks, R.F., 'Key Issues in Criminology', Weidenfeld & Nicolson, 1970, ch. 6.

36 West, D.J., 'The Habitual Prisoner', Macmillan, 1963.

37 Rapaport, L., Crisis Intervention as a Mode of Treatment, in Roberts, R. and Nee, R. (eds), 'Theories of Social Casework', University of Chicago Press, 1970, p. 302.

38 Allen, op. cit., pp. 231-2.

39 Ibid., p. 232.

40 Matza, D., 'Delinquency and Drift', Wiley, 1964, pp. 115-16

41 Ibid.

Chapter 4   Treatment and the experts

1 Packer, Herbert L., 'The Limits of the Criminal Sanction', Oxford University Press, 1969.

2 Ibid., p. 26.

3 Goffman, E., 'Asylums', Penguin, 1961, p. 146.

4 Probation Officers are under considerable pressure from middle class clients to operate on a special privilege basis. Middle class offenders resent sitting in waiting rooms with other offenders, thereby implying that probation is after

all directed at the working classes.

5   de Berker, P., The Inadequate Personality, 'British Journal of Criminology', July 1960. See also de Berker, P. and P., 'Misfits', Pitman, 1973, pp. 112, 113.
6   Goffman, E., op. cit., p. 145.
7   Ibid., p. 318.
8   See Young, J., 'The Drug Takers', Paladin, 1971 for a discussion on psychiatric practices and social controls.
9   Hadden, T.B., A Plea for Punishment, 'Cambridge Law Journal', April 1965, p. 124.
10 Lewis, C. S., A Plea for Punishment in Radzinowicz, L. and Wolfgang, M. (eds), 'Crime and Justice', Basic Books, 1971, vol. 2.
11 Gusfield, Joseph, Moral Passage, in Bersani, C. (ed.), 'Crime and Delinquency', Macmillan, 1970.
12 Berlin. I., 'Four Essays on Liberty', Oxford University Press, 1969.
13 HMSO 'Report of the Work of the Probation and After-Care Service, 1969-71', Cmd 5158.
14 Jarvis, F., 'Manual of Probation', Butterworth, 1969.
15 Miles, Arthur, The Utility of Case Records, in Carter, R.M., and Wilkins, L.T. (eds), 'Probation and Parole', Wiley, 1970.
16 Quoted by Gronewold, D., Supervision Practices in the Federal Probation System, in Carter, R.M. and Wilkins, L.T., op. cit., p. 307.
17 Wheeler, Stanton, 'On Record', Russell Sage Foundation, 1969.
18 See particularly Cicourel, A.V., 'The Social Organisation of Juvenile Justice', Wiley, 1968 for an account of how records became truncated versions of 'what happened'.
19 Davies, Martin and Knopf, Andrea, 'Social Enquiry Reports and the Probation Service', HMSO, 1973, p. 12.
20 Sparks, R.F., 'Research on the Use and Effectiveness of Probation, Parole and Measures of After-Care', Council of Europe, 1968.
21 Ibid.
22 Davies, Martin and Knopf, Andrea, op. cit.
23 California Board of Correction, Special Intensive Parole Unit, Phase 3, 'Research Report No. 3,' March 1962.
24 Davies, M. and Chapman, B., Change of Supervising Officer and Commission of Further Offences, Case Conference, November 1969, vol. 16, no. 7, pp. 250-3.
25 HMSO 'The Sentence of the Court'. See also Wilkins, L.T., A Small Comparative Study of the Results of Probation, 'British Journal of Delinquency', 1968, vol. 8, p. 201, for a comparison between probation and imprisonment.
26 Grunhut, M., 'Probation and Mental Treatment', Tavistock, 1963.
27 Goffman, E., op. cit., p. 144.
28 Rollin, Henry R., 'The Mentally Abnormal Offender and the Law', Pergamon (Commonwealth and International Library), 1969.
29 Walker, N. and McCabe, S., 'Crime and Insanity in England', Edinburgh University Press, vol. 2, 1973, p. 166.
30 Ibid., p. 126.
31 Ibid., p. 126.
32 Ibid., p. 155.
33 Walker, Nigel, 'Crime and Punishment in Britain', Edinburgh University Press, 1968, p. 257.
34 See also Williams, D., The Police and Law Enforcement, 'Criminal Law Review', 1968, pp. 351-62.
35 Gittens, J., 'Approved School Boys', HMSO, 1952, p. 15.

36   Ibid., p. 40.
37   Morrison, R.L., Borstal Allocation, 'British Journal of Delinquency',
      1957, vol. 8., pp. 95-105.
38   Ibid., p. 40.
39   Fisher, R., The Assessment of the Effects on English Borstal Boys of
      Different Correctional Training and Treatment Problems, unpublished
      Ph. D. thesis, London School of Economics, 1967.

Chapter 5   Sentencing and the social enquiry report

1   'Royal Commission on the Penal System', HMSO, 1967, vol. 2, pp. 93,
      152, 179.
2   Matza, D., 'Delinquency and Drift', Wiley, 1964, p. 114.
3   Glueck, S., quoted by Barry, Sir J., Judicial Sentencing or Treatment
      Tribunals, in Radzinowicz, L. and Wolfgang, M. (eds), 'Crime and Justice',
      Basic Books, 1971, vol. 2, pp. 662-3.
4   Morris, Norval, Address given to Eighth Legal Convention of the Law
      Council in Australia, in Radzinowicz, L. and Wolfgang, M., op. cit., p. 660.
5   For the best discussion on disparities see Hood, R.G., 'Sentencing in
      Magistrates' Courts', Stevens, 1962. Also see Hood, R.G. and Sparks, R.F.,
      'Key Issues in Criminology', Weidenfeld & Nicolson, 1970, pp. 142-52,
      for a summary of recent research.
6   Hogarth, John, 'Sentencing as a Human Process', Toronto University Press,
      1971.
7   'Royal Commission on the Penal System', vol. 2, p. 127.
8   Calculations are based on the figures given in HMSO, 'Report of the Work
      of the Probation and After-Care Department', Cmd 5158.
9   Sparks, R.F., Sentencing by Magistrates, in Halmos, P. (ed.) Sociological
      Studies in the British Penal Services, 'Sociological Review Monograph,
      No. 9', 1965, pp. 72-3.
10   Walker, Nigel, 'Crime and Punishment in Britain', Edinburgh University
      Press, 1968, p. 232.
11   Borstal sentences and extended sentences involve these two elements.
12   See Mathieson, D.A. and Walker, A.J., Probation Papers No. 7,
      NAPO 1971. The authors believe that 'the time cannot be too distant'
      when sentencing panels will be introduced for selected types of offenders
      such as persistent offenders and those requiring medical treatment.
13   See also Bean, Philip, The Challenge of Social Enquiry Reports, 'Family
      Law', February 1974, vol. 4, no. 1, pp. 25-8.
14   Thomas, D., Theories of Punishment in the Court of Appeal, 'Modern Law
      Review', 1964, vol. 27.
15   See also Thomas, D.A., 'Sentencing: the Basic Principles', Heinemann,
      1970.
16   Hogarth, John, op. cit.
17   McClintock, F.H., 'Crimes of Violence', Macmillan, 1963, p. 166.
18   Radzinowicz, L., 'Sexual Offences', Macmillan, 1957, p. 191.
19   Hood, R.G., 'Sentencing the Motoring Offender', Heinemann, 1972.
20   Bean, Philip, Social Aspects of Drug Abuse, 'Journal of Criminal Law,
      Criminology and Police Science', 1971, vol. 62, no. 1.
21   Hood, R.G., 'Sentencing in Magistrates' Courts', op. cit.
22   Hogarth, John, op. cit., p. 159.
23   Wheeler, Stanton, Agents of Delinquency Control, in Wheeler, S. (ed.),
      'Controlling Delinquents', Wiley, 1968.

24   Allen, Francis A., Criminal Justice, Legal Values, and the Rehabilitative Ideal, 'Journal of Criminal Law, Criminology and Police Science', 1959, vol. 50, p. 231.
25   Various Home Office circulars have extended the range of SERs. The most important ones were in 1963 and 1968. The 1963 circular (138/1963) endorsed the recommendation of the Streatfeild Committee, which suggested that higher courts should consider reports:
1   On all offenders under 30.
2   On all offenders with no previous convictions who had committed offences for which they could be sent to prison.
3   On all offenders recently in contact with the probation service (paras 355-61).
These categories were minimum ones which could equally apply to the Magistrates' Courts. The 1967 Criminal Justice Act (Sec. 57) gave the Home Secretary powers to require courts to consider an SER before passing a custodial sentence. No rules have been made as yet but in 1968 the Home Office issued another circular which recommended that:
1   All courts to consider an SER before sentencing anyone over 17 to a custodial sentence for 2 years or less where the offender has had no previous custodial sentence. This includes Borstal, Detention Centres, prison and suspended sentence.
2   Before sentencing any women to prison.
3   Before committing a person to a higher court for sentence.
4   Where juveniles appear in Magistrates' Courts convicted with an older offender before the courts made a Care Order.
26   HMSO Report of the Work of the Probation and After-Care Service, HOC 59/1971 provides an up to date account of all previous circulars. There are of course numerous other reports which have not been considered here. These include Divorce Court welfare reports, matrimonial reports, means enquiries, adoption reports, etc. They are not included because they are not, strictly speaking, part of the penal system but part of civil law. Neither have I included reports on offenders sentenced to life imprisonment. HOC 171/1968.
27   HMSO 'Report on the Work of the Prison Department', 1971, Cmd 5037, p. 64.
28   HMSO 'Report of the Interdepartmental Committee on the Business of the Criminal Courts' 1962, Cmd 1289.
29   Ibid., paras 336, 337.
30   Mathieson, D.A. and Walker, A.J., op. cit.
31   Op. cit., para. 336.
32   HMSO 'The Sentence of the Court', 1969.
33   HMSO 'Report of the Interdepartmental Committee on the Business of the Criminal Courts', para. 92.
34   Hogarth, John, Towards the Improvement of Sentencing in Canada, 'Canadian Journal of Corrections', 1967, vol. 9, no. 2, p. 130.
35   Blumberg, A.S., 'Criminal Justice', Quadrangle Books, 1967.
36   Probation Officers are asked to send a copy of their report to the psychiatrist before the psychiatrist interviews the offender.
37   Mathieson, D.A. and Walker, A.J., op. cit., p. 7.
38   Ibid.
39   Szasz, T., 'The Myth of Mental Illness', Paladin, 1972, p. 270.
40   Davies, Martin and Knopf, Andrea, 'Social Enquiry Reports and the Probation Service' HMSO, no. 18, 1973. See also Perry, F.G., 'Information for the Court', University of Cambridge, Institute of Criminology, 1964.

41 Cicourel, A.V., 'The Social Organization of Juvenile Justice', Wiley, 1968.
42 Bean, Philip, Social Enquiry Reports and the Decision Making Process, 'Family Law', 1971, vol. 1, no. 6, p. 174.
43 Erikson, Kai and Gilberton, D., Case Records in a Mental Hospital, in Wheeler, Stanton (ed.), 'On Record', Russell Sage Foundation, 1969, pp. 403-4.
44 A large scale research study of this issue is currently being prepared by Pauline Hardiker, University of Leicester.
45 Carter, R.M., The Pre-sentence Report and the Decision Making Process, in Carter, R.M. and Wilkins, L.T. (eds), 'Probation and Parole', Wiley, 1970.
46 Op. cit., para. 346.
47 Few psychiatrists have much knowledge about the penal system. On one occasion, the author was asked by a consultant psychiatrist who claimed to have written hundreds of reports, if there was any difference between a detention centre and borstal!
48 Op. cit., para. 339.
49 HMSO 'Report of the Departmental Committee on the Probation Service', 1962, Cmd 1650, para. 41.
50 Ford, Peter, 'Advising Sentencers', Blackwell, 1972.
51 Op. cit., p. 36.
52 'Justice of the Peace', 1967, vol. 131, no. 49, p. 785.
53 Jarvis, F.V., Inquiry before Sentence, in Grygier, T., et al. (eds), 'Criminology in Transition', Tavistock, 1965, pp. 43-63.
54 San Francisco Project, Report No. 2, 1965.
55 This interesting phrase is reported by Peter Ford and it conveys a wealth of information about the relationship between the probation service and the courts.
56 Emerson, Robert M., 'Judging Delinquents', Aldine, 1969, p. 124.
57 Ibid., p. 170.
58 See Plotnikoff, J. for a discussion on some of the legal implications of pre-trial reports, 'British Journal of Social Work', 1973, vol. 3, no. 2.
59 Blumberg, A.S., op. cit., p. 146.

Chapter 6   Rehabilitation in penal institutions

1 The average population in 1972 fell by about 4 per cent over 1971, the largest absolute reduction coming from the adult male group. Of the 38,328 in custody there were 24,534 sentenced adult prisoners (aged 21 or over) and a further 1,353 young prisoners (aged 17-21). The remainder included 1,738 in detention centres, 5,509 in borstals, 497 civil prisoners and 4,697 were awaiting trial or sentence. Custodial sentences account for 12 per cent of all sentences passed and just over 60 per cent of all custodial sentences are for 6 months or less. See HMSO 'Report on the Work of the Prison Department', 1973.
2 American Correctional Association, Development of Modern Correctional Concepts and Standards, in Carter, R.M., Glaser, D. and Wilkins, L.T. (eds), 'Correctional Institutions', Lippincott, 1972, pp. 33-4.
3 HMSO, 'People in Prison', 1969, Cmd 4214, p. 26.
4 Ibid.
5 King, Roy D. and Cooper, M., Social and Economic Problems of Prisoners' Work, in Halmos, P. (ed.), 'Sociological studies of the British Penal Services', Sociological Review Monograph no. 9, 1965.
6 'People in Prison', op. cit., para. 47.

7   See Zeno, 'Life', Macmillan, 1968, for his account of how he protected himself as a prisoner against the social failures, or as he called them 'the unloved'.

8   Op. cit., para. 13. See also Bottomley, A. Keith, 'Decisions in the Penal Process', Martin Robertson, 1973, p. 173.

9   Fox, Sir. L., quoted by Morrison, R.L., in his paper to the British Congress on crime, 1967, p. 85.

10 Morrison, R.L., ibid., discusses this point.

11 Incidentally the HMSO document 'People in Prison' makes it clear that a court may pass a sentence for varying ideological reasons but this does not affect the duty of the prison service whose major aim is still security.

12 Schrag, C., Some Foundations for a Theory of Corrections, in Cressey, D. R. (ed.), 'The Prison', Holt, Rinehart & Winston, 1961.

13 Morris, T. and P., 'Pentonville', Routledge & Kegan Paul, 1963.

14 Clemmer, D., 'The Prison Community', Holt, Rinehart & Winston, 1958. This passage quoted by Hood, R.G. and Sparks, R.F., 'Key Issues in Criminology', Weidenfeld & Nicolson, 1970, p. 218.

15 Sykes, G. and Messinger, S., The Inmate Social System, in Grosser, G. (ed.) 'Theoretical Studies in the Social Organisation of the Prison', SSRC, 1960, pp. 5-11.

16 See Sykes, G., 'The Society of Captives', Princeton University Press, 1971, p. 107.

17 Irwin, J. and Cressey, D., Thieves, Convicts and the Inmate Subculture, 'Social Problems', 1962, vol. 10, p. 42.

18 Morris, T. and P., op. cit., p. 230.

19 Hood, R.G. and Sparks, R.F., 'Key Issues in Criminology', Weidenfeld & Nicolson, 1970, ch. 8. This chapter provides a first class summary of most of the sociological research in prisons.

20 Clemmer, D., op. cit., p. 300.

21 See particularly Wheeler, S., Role Conflict in Correctional Communities, in Cressey, D. (ed.), 'The Prison', Holt, Rinehart & Winston, 1961.

22 Polsky, Howard 'Cottage Six', Russell Sage Foundation, 1962.

23 Mathiesen, T., 'The Defences of the Weak', Tavistock, 1965, pp. 195-200.

24 Bottomley, A.Keith, op. cit., p. 177.

25 Thomas, J.E., 'The English Prison Officer since 1850', Routledge & Kegan Paul, 1972, p. 2.

26 Bottomley, A. Keith, op. cit., p. 177.

27 HMSO 'Report of the Inquiry into Prison Escapes and Security', 1966, Cmd 3175.

28 Morris, T. and P., op. cit., p. 99.

29 Driscoll, A.W., Key Men, 'Prison Service Journal', 1966, vol. 5, no. 20, pp. 2-7.

30 Ibid., p. 7.

31 Glaser, D., 'The Effectiveness of a Prison and Parole System', Bobbs-Merrill, 1964, p. 147.

32 Both quotes taken from 'Prison Officers' Magazine', November 1963, p. 332 and February 1966, p. 28.

33 Jarvis, F., The Prison Welfare Service, 'Probation', March 1967, vol. 13, no. 1, p. 8.

34 Morrison, R.L., Individualization and Involvement in Treatment and Prevention, in Klare, H.J. and Haxby, D.A. (eds), 'Frontiers of Criminology', Pergamon, 1967, pp. 85-102.

35 Conrad, J.P., 'Crime and its Correction', Tavistock, 1965, p. 238.

36 Groupwork in prisons began in Folsom Prison, California in 1954 and was

introduced to reduce conflict in a maximum security prison well known for its violence. It was therefore an organizational expedient. Folsom Prison had a high intake of violent prisoners but the effect of groupwork was immediate and violence was reduced (ibid.). The Home Office in 1962 was satisfied that groupwork had considerable value and planned a modest extension of its use. See Home Office Circular 'Group Counselling', HOC 62/62, 2 May, 1962.

37 See Thomas, J.E., After Care and the Prison Officer, 'Prison Service Journal', July 1965, vol. 4, no. 16, p. 19.

38 HMSO Minutes of Evidence taken before the Sub-Committes on Social Affairs, in 'Eleventh Report of Estimates Committee', Session 1966-7, p. 182.

39 HMSO 'Report on the Work of the Prison Department', 1972, Cmd 5375, para. 100.

40 James, H., After-Care as seen by a Principal Probation Officer, 'Contact', November 1965, p. 14; James worked out that 100 PWOs with 30,000 prisoners gives each prisoner 6 hours of PWO's time per year.

41 See Stanley, A.R., Casework in a Local Prison, 'Probation', November 1966, vol. 12. no. 3, p. 91.

42 Morris, Pauline, Trends in the Probation and After-Care Service, 'Probation', November 1966, vol. 12, no. 3.

43 Morrison, R.L., Casework in an institutional setting, papers read at Principal Probation Officers' Conference, York, 1966, mimeo.

44 HMSO 'Report on Discharged Prisoners' Aid Societies' (Maxwell Committee), 1951, Cmd 8879, para. 76.

45 HMSO 'The Organisation of After Care', 1963, para. 21.

46 Jones, Howard, Prison Officers as Therapists, 'Howard Journal', 1966, vol. 12.

47 Shapland, P., Short Sentence Recidivist Groups and After-Care, 'Prison Service Journal', vol. 5, no. 40, 1966.

48 HMSO 'Explorations in After-Care', 1971, no. 9, pp. 29-30.

49 Ibid., p. 44.

50 Mathiesen, T., op. cit., p. 23.

Chapter 7   A personal overview

1 Davis, K., 'Discretionary Justice', Baton Rouge, 1969, p. 3.

2 See also Bottomley, A. Keith, 'Decisions in the Penal Process', Martin Robertson, 1973, p. 220.

3 In fact some courts insist that probation officers read the reports out to the courts, but medical reports are outside this ruling. Perhaps they have more mystique.

4 Lewis, C.S., quoted by Prins, Hershel, Motivation in Social Work, 'Social Work Today', vol. 5., no. 2, p. 42, 1974.

5 Ibid., p. 42.

Selected reading

Allen, Francis A., Criminal Justice, Legal Values and the Rehabilitative Ideal, 'Journal of Criminal Law, Criminology and Police Science', 1959, vol. 50, pp. 226-32.

Allen, Francis A., 'The Borderland of Criminal Justice', University of Chicago Press, 1964.

Anttila, I., Conservative and Radical Criminal Policy in Nordic Countries, 'Scandinavian Studies in Criminology', 1971, vol. 3.

Blumberg, A.S., 'Criminal Justice', Quadrangle Books, 1967.

Bottomley, A. Keith, 'Decisions in the Penal Process', Martin Robertson, 1973.

Davis, K.C., 'Discretionary Justice', Baton Rouge, 1969.

Emerson, Robert M., 'Judging Delinquents', Aldine, 1969.

Flew, Anthony, 'Crime or Disease', Macmillan, 1973.

Ford, Peter, 'Advising Sentencers', Blackwell, 1972.

Goffman, E., 'Asylums', Penguin, 1961.

Hadden, T.B., A Plea for Punishment, 'Cambridge Law Journal', April 1965.

Hogarth, J., Towards the Improvement of Sentencing in Canada, 'Canadian Journal of Corrections', 1967, vol. 9.

Jeffrey, C.R., Positivism and the Classical School, in Mannheim, H. (ed.) 'Pioneers in Criminology', Stevens, 1960.

Kittrie, Nicholas N., 'The Right to be Different', Johns Hopkins Press, 1971.

Lemert, Edwin M., 'Human Deviance, Social Problems and Social Control', Prentice-Hall, 1967.

Lemert, Edwin M., 'Social Action and Legal Change', Aldine, 1970.

Lewis, C.S., The Humanitarian Theory of Punishment, in Radzinowicz, L. and Wolfgang, M. (eds), 'Crime and Justice', Basic Books, 1971, vol. 2.

Mathiesen, T., 'The Defences of the Weak', Tavistock, 1965.

Matza, D., 'Delinquency and Drift', Wiley 1964.

Mills, C. Wright, The Professional Ideology of Social Pathologists, 'American Journal of Sociology', 1943, vol. 49, no. 2, pp. 165-80.

Packer, Herbert L., 'The Limits of the Criminal Sanction', Oxford University Press, 1969.

Schur, Edwin M., 'Radical Non-Intervention', Prentice-Hall, 1973.

159

Steadman, H., The Psychiatrist as a Conservative Agent of Social Control, 'Social Problems', 1972, vol. 20, no. 2.

Szasz, T., Psychiatric Expert Testimony,'Psychiatry', 1957, vol. 20.

Szasz, T., Moral Conflict and Psychiatry, 'Yale Review', Summer 1960, vol. 49.

Szasz, T., 'Law, Liberty and Psychiatry', Routledge & Kegan Paul, 1974.

Thomas, J.E., 'The English Prison Officer since 1850', Routledge & Kegan Paul, 1972.

White, R., Lawyers and the Enforcement of Rights, in Morris, Pauline et al., 'Social Needs and Legal Action', Martin Robertson, 1973.

Wootton, B., 'Social Science and Social Pathology', Allen & Unwin, 1960.

Wootton, B., The Law, the Doctor and the Deviant, 'British Medical Journal', 21 July 1963.

Bibliography

American Correctional Association, Development of Modern Correctional
Concepts and Standards, in Carter, R.M., Glaser, D. and Wilkins, L.T. (1972).
Aubert, V. (ed.), 'Sociology of Law', Penguin, 1969.
Barry, Sir J., Judicial Sentencing or Treatment Tribunals, in Radzinowicz, L. and
Wolfgang, M. (1971).
Bean, Philip, Social Aspects of Drug Abuse, 'Journal of Criminal Law, Criminology
and Police Science', 1971, vol. 62, no. 1.
Bean, Philip, Social Enquiry Reports and the Decision Making Process, 'Family
Law', 1971, vol. 1, no. 6.
Bean, Philip, The Challenge of Social Enquiry Reports, 'Family Law', 1974, vol.4, no.1.
Bean, Philip, 'The Social Control of Drugs', Martin Robertson, 1974.
Becker, Howard S., 'The Other Side', Free Press, 1964.
Bendix, R., 'Max Weber, an Intellectual Portrait', Doubleday, 1960.
Benn, S.I. and Peters, R.S., 'Social Principles and the Democratic State',
Allen & Unwin, 1959.
Berger, P. and Luckmann, T., 'The Social Construction of Reality', Allen Lane,
1967.
de Berker, P., The Inadequate Personality, 'British Journal of Criminology', July
1960.
de Berker, P. and P., 'Misfits', Pitman, 1973.
Berlin, I., 'Four Essays on Liberty', Oxford University Press, 1969.
Bredemeur, H., Law and Social Structure in Aubert, V. (1969).
Briar, S. and Miller, H., 'Problems and Issues in Social Casework', Columbia
University Press, 1971.
California Board of Corrections Special Intensive Parole Unit, Phase 3,
'Research Report No. 3', March 1962.
California Board of Corrections, San Francisco Project Research Report No. 11
'The Intensive Supervision Caseload', 1967.
Carter, R.M., The Pre-sentence Report and the Decision Making Process, in Carter,
R.M. and Wilkins, L.T. (1970).
Carter, R.M., Glaser, D. and Wilkins, L.T. (eds), 'Correctional Institutions'
Lippincott, 1972.

161

Carter, R.M. and Wilkins, L.T. (eds), 'Probation and Parole', Wiley, 1970.
Carter, R.M. and Wilkins, L.T., Some Factors in Sentencing Policy, in Carter, R.M. and Wilkins, L.T. (1970).
Chambliss, W., The Law of Vagrancy, in Chambliss, W. (ed.), 'Crime and the Legal Process', McGraw-Hill, 1969.
Chapman, D., 'Sociology and the Stereotype of the Criminal', Tavistock, 1968.
Cicourel, A.V., 'The Social Organization of Juvenile Justice', Wiley, 1968.
Clemmer, D., 'The Prison Community', Holt, Rinehart & Winston, 1958.
Cloward, R.A., Social Control in the Prison, in Social Science Research Council, 'Studies in the Social Organization of the Prison', 1960.
Cohen, Stanley, Criminology and the Sociology of Deviance in Britain, in Rock, Paul and McIntosh, Mary (eds), 'Deviance and Social Control', Tavistock, 1974.
Conrad, J.P., 'Crime and its Correction', Tavistock, 1965.
Cressey, D. (ed.) 'The Prison', Holt, Rinehart & Winston, 1966.
Davies, Martin, Social Inquiry for the Courts, 'British Journal of Criminology', 1974, vol. 14, no. 1.
Davies, Martin and Knopf, Andrea, 'Social Enquiry Reports and the Probation Service', HMSO, 1973.
Dicey, A., Law and Public Opinion, in Aubert, V. (1969).
Driscoll, A.W., Key Men, 'Prison Service Journal', 1966, vol. 5, no. 20.
Durkheim, E., 'The Division of Labour in Society', Free Press, 1964.
Erickson, Kai, Notes on the Sociology of Deviance, in Becker, Howard S., (1974).
Erickson, Kai and Gilberton, D., Case Records in a Mental Hospital, in Wheeler, Stanton (1969).
Fabrega, H. and Manning, P., Disease, Illness and Deviant Careers, in Scott, R. and Douglas, J. (1972).
Fisher, R., The Assessment of the Effects on English Borstal Boys of Different Correctional Training and Treatment Problems, unpublished Ph. D. Thesis, London School of Economics, 1967.
Garfinkel, H., Conditions of Successful Degradation Ceremonies, 'American Journal of Sociology', 1956, vol. 61.
Garrity, Donald L., The Prison as a Rehabilitation Agency, in Cressey, D. (1966).
Gittens, J., 'Approved School Boys', HMSO, 1952.
Glaser, D., 'The Effectiveness of a Prison and Parole System', Bobbs-Merrill, 1964.
Glaser, Daniel and Stratton, John R., Measuring Inmate Change, in Cressey, D. (1966).
Glueck, S., 'Laws and Psychiatry', Johns Hopkins Press, 1962.
Gronewold, D., Supervision Practices in the Federal Probation System, in Carter, R.M. and Wilkins, L.T. (1970).
Grunhut, M., 'Probation and Mental Treatment', Tavistock, 1963.
Gurvitch, G., 'Sociology of Law', Routledge & Kegan Paul, 1973.
Gusfield, Joseph, Moral Passage, in Bersani, C. (ed.), 'Crime and Delinquency', Macmillan, 1970.
Hadden, T. and McClintock, F., 'Social and Legal Definitions of Criminal Violence', Fourth National Conference on Research and Teaching in Criminology, Institute of Criminology, Cambridge, 1970.
Hardiker, Pauline, 'Research on Social Enquiry Reports', University of Leicester (in preparation).
HMSO, 'Report of the Departmental Committee on Prisons' (Gladstone Report) 1895, Cmd 7703.
HMSO, 'Report on Discharged Prisoners' Aid Societies' (Maxwell Committee), 1951, Cmd 8879.
HMSO, 'Report of the Interdepartmental Committee on the Business of the Criminal Courts' (Streatfeild Committee), 1962, Cmd 1289.

HMSO, 'Group Counselling', HOC 62/62.
HMSO, 'Report of the Departmental Committee on the Probation Service', 1962, Cmd 1650.
HMSO, 'The Organization of After-Care' (ACTO), 1963.
HMSO, 'Prison Officers' Magazine', November 1963.
HMSO, 'Prison Service Journal', 1965, vol. 14, no. 16.
HMSO, 'Minutes of Evidence taken before the Sub-Committee on Social Affairs in Eleventh Report of Estimates Committee, Session 1966/7'.
HMSO, 'Preliminary Report on the Probation Research Project', 1966.
HMSO, 'Prison Service Journal', 1966, vol. 15, no. 20.
HMSO, 'Report of the Inquiry into Prison Escapes and Security', 1966, Cmd 3175.
HMSO, HOC 130/67, 'The Role and Functions of the Prison Welfare Officer'.
HMSO, 'Royal Commission on the Penal System', vols 1, 2, 3, and 4, 1967.
HMSO, HOC 171/68.
HMSO, 'People in Prison', 1969, Cmd 4214.
HMSO, 'Report of the Work of the Probation and After-Care Department, 1969-71', Cmd 5158.
HMSO, 'The Sentence of the Court', 1969.
HMSO, 'Explorations in After-Care', 1971, no. 9.
HMSO, HOC 59/71.
HMSO, 'Report on the Work of the Prison Department', 1971, Cmd 5037.
HMSO, 'Report of the Work of the Prison Department' 1972, Cmd 5375.
HMSO, 'Social Enquiry Reports and the Probation Service', 1973, no. 18.
Hogarth, John, 'Sentencing as a Human Process', Toronto University Press, 1971.
Holloway, V., The Future of Classification, in Klare, H.J. and Haxby, D.A., 'Frontiers of Criminology', Pergamon, 1967.
Hood, R.G., 'Sentencing in Magistrates' Courts', Stevens, 1962.
Hood, R.G., 'Homeless Borstal Boys', Bell, 1966.
Hood, R.G., 'Sentencing the Motoring Offender', Heinemann, 1972.
Hood, R.G., and Sparks, R.F., 'Key Issues in Criminology', Weidenfeld & Nicolson, 1970.
Hood, R.G. and Taylor, Ian, The Effectiveness of Presentence Investigations in Reducing Recidivism, 'British Journal of Criminology', 1968, vol. 8, no. 4.
Irwin, J. and Cressey, D., Thieves. Convicts and the Inmate Subculture, 'Social Problems', 1962, vol. 10.
Jackson, George, 'Soledad Brother', Jonathan Cape/Penguin, 1971.
James, H., After-Care as seen by a Principal Probation Officer. 'Contact', November, 1965.
Jarvis, F., Inquiry before Sentence, in Grygier, T. et al. (eds), 'Criminology in Transition', Tavistock, 1965.
Jarvis, F., The Prison Welfare Service, 'Probation', 1967, vol. 13, no. 1.
Jarvis, F., 'Manual of Probation', Butterworth, 1969.
Jones, H., Prison Officers as Therapists, 'Howard Journal', 1966, vol. 12.
'Justice of the Peace' (editorial comment), 1967, vol. 131, no. 49.
King, Roy D. and Cooper, M., Social and Economic Problems of Prisoners' Work, in Halmos, P. (ed.), Sociological Studies in the British Penal Services, 'Sociological Review Monograph no. 9', 1965.
Kutchinsky, Berl, The Legal Consciousness, in Podgorecki, A. et al. (eds), 'Knowledge and Opinion about Law', Martin Robertson, 1973.
Lerman, Paul, 'Delinquency and Social Policy', Praeger, 1970.
Lopez-Rey, M., 'Crime: An Analytical Appraisal', Routledge & Kegan Paul, 1970.
Lukes, Steven, 'Emile Durkheim:, His Life and Work', Allen Lane, 1973.
McClean J.D. and Wood J.C., 'Criminal Justice and the Treatment of Offenders',

163

Bibliography

Sweet & Maxwell, 1969.

McClintock, F.H., 'Crimes of Violence', Macmillan, 1963.

McGarry, A., The Fate of Psychotic Offenders Returned to Trial, 'American Journal of Psychiatry', 1971, vol. 127.

Mannheim, H. (ed.), 'Pioneers in Criminology', Stevens, 1960.

Mathieson, D.A. and Walker, A.J., Social Enquiry Reports, Probation Papers, no. 7, NAPO 1971.

Miles, Arthur, The Utility of Case Records, in Carter, R.M. and Wilkins, L.T. (1970).

Mill, J.S., 'On Liberty', Blackwell, 1946.

Moberley, Sir W., 'The Ethics of Punishment', Faber, 1968.

Monger, Mark, 'Casework in After-Care', Butterworth, 1967.

Morris, Norval, Address given to the Eighth Legal Convention of the Law Council in Australia, in Radzinowicz, L. and Wolfgang, M. (1971).

Morris, Pauline, Trends in the Probation and After-Care Service, 'Probation', November 1966, vol. 12, no. 3.

Morris, Pauline, White, Richard and Lewis, Philip, 'Social Needs and Legal Action', Martin Robertson, 1973.

Morris, Terence and Pauline, 'Pentonville', Routledge & Kegan Paul, 1963.

Morrison R.L., Borstal Allocation, 'British Journal of Delinquency', 1957, vol. 8.

Morrison, R.L., Authority and Treatment, in 'The Concepts of Authority', Shotton Hall Publications, 1966.

Morrison, R.L., Individualization and Involvement in Treatment and Prevention, in Klare, H.J. and Haxby, D.A. (eds) 'Frontiers in Criminology', Pergamon, 1967.

Parsons, Talcott, 'The Social System', Free Press, 1951.

Parsons, T. and Smelser, N., 'Economy and Society', Free Press, 1956.

Perry, F.G., 'Information for the Court', University of Cambridge, Institute of Criminology, 1974.

Plotnikoff, J., A Problem for Law and Social Work, 'British Journal of Social Work', 1973, vol. 3, no. 2.

Polsky, H.W., 'Cottage Six', Russell Sage Foundation, 1962.

Prins, Herschel, Motivation in Social Work, 'Social Work Today', 1974, vol. 5, no. 2.

Prins, Herschel, 'Criminal Behaviour', Pitman, 1974.

Radzinowicz, L., 'Sexual Offences', Macmillan, 1957.

Radzinowicz, L. and Wolfgang, M., 'Crime and Justice', Basic Books, 1971, vol. 2.

Rapaport, L., Crisis Intervention as a Mode of Treatment, in Roberts, R. and Nee, R. (eds), 'Theories of Social Casework', University of Chicago Press, 1970.

Rollin, Henry R., 'The Mentally Abnormal Offender and the Law', Pergamon (Commonwealth and International Library), 1969.

Rosenburg, A. and McGarry, L., Competency for Trial, the Making of an Expert, 'American Journal of Psychiatry', March 1972, vol. 128.

Schrag, C., Leadership among prison inmates, 'American Sociological Review', February 1954.

Schrag, C., Some Foundations for a Theory of Corrections, in Cressey, D.R. (1966).

Schur, Edwin, M., 'Radical Non-Intervention', Prentice-Hall, 1973.

Scott, R. and Douglas, J. (eds), 'Theoretical Perspectives on Deviance', Basic Books, 1972.

Shapland, P., Short Sentence Recidivist Groups and After Care, 'Prison Service Journal', 1966, vol. 5, no. 40.

Smith, John, Guilty without Intent, 'New Society', 14 April 1969.

Smith, S., 'Social Pathology', Macmillan, 1911.

Sparks, R.F., Sentencing by Magistrates, in Halmos, P. (ed.), Sociological studies in the British Penal Services, 'Sociological Review Monograph, no. 9', 1965.
Sparks, R.F., 'Research on the Use and Effectiveness of Probation Parole and Measures of After-Care', Council of Europe, 1968.
Sparks, R.F., The Depraved are not just Deprived, 'New Society', 24 July 1969.
Stanley, A.R., Casework in a Local Prison. 'Probation', November 1966, vol. 12, no. 3.
Sykes, G., 'The Society of Captives', Princeton University Press, 1958.
Sykes, G. and Messinger, S., The inmate social system, in Grosser, G. (ed.), 'Theoretical Studies in the Social Organization of the Prison', Social Science Research Council, 1960.
Taylor, I., Walton, P. and Young, J., 'The New Criminology', Routledge & Kegan Paul, 1973.
Thomas, D.A., Theories of Punishment in the Court of Appeal, 'Modern Law Review', 1964, vol. 27.
Thomas, D.A., 'Sentencing: the Basic Principles', Heinemann, 1970.
Thomas, J.E., The Prison Officer's Role, 'The Criminologist', May 1968, vol. 8.
Van Houtte, J. and Vinke, P., Attitudes governing the acceptance of Legislation in Various Countries, in Podgorecki, A. et al. (eds), 'Knowledge and Opinion about Law', Martin Robertson, 1973.
Walker, Nigel, 'Crime and Punishment in Britain', Edinburgh University Press, 1968.
Walker, Nigel, 'Sentencing in a Rational Society', Allen Lane, 1972.
Walker, Nigel and McCabe, Sarah, 'Crime and Insanity in England', Edinburgh University Press, 1973, vol. 2.
Weber, Max, 'Law in Society', Harvard University Press, 1954.
Weber, Max, 'The City', Free Press, 1958.
Weber, Max, 'The Theory of Social and Economic Organization', Free Press, 1964.
Weinberg, M. and Rubington, E. (eds), 'The Solution of Social Problems', Oxford University Press, 1973.
Weschsler H., Law, Morals and Society, 'Columbia Law School News', 2 April 1959, vol. 13.
West, D.J., 'The Habitual Prisoner', Macmillan, 1963.
Wheeler, Stanton, Agents of Delinquency Control, in Wheeler, S. (ed.), 'Controlling Delinquents', Wiley, 1968.
Wheeler, Stanton (ed.), 'On Record', Russell Sage Foundation, 1969.
Wheeler, Stanton, Socialization in Correctional Institutions, in Radzinowicz, L. and Wolfgang, M., 'Crime and Justice', Basic Books, vol. 3, 1971.
Wilkins, L.T., A Small Comparative Study of the Results of Probation, 'British Journal of Delinquency', 1968. vol. 8.
Williams, D., The Police and Law Enforcement, 'Criminal Law Review', August 1968, pp. 351-62.
Young, J., 'The Drug Takers', Paladin, 1971.
Zeno, 'Life', Macmillan, 1968.

Index

Radical Social Policy

GENERAL EDITOR

Vic George

*Professor of Social Policy and
Administration and Social Work
University of Kent*

Rehabilitation and deviance

WITHDRAWN